HARMONY

BY Diane Blacker
*Totally New
Harmony*

HARMONY

How to Let God's Gifts Come Together in Your Life

DIANE BLACKER

Fleming H. Revell Company
Old Tappan, New Jersey

Library of Congress Cataloging in Publication Data

Blacker, Diane.

    Harmony

    Bibliography: p.
    1. Christian life—1960—   I. Title.
BV4501.2.B538   248!.4   77-28033
ISBN 0-8007-0900-4

TO my mother, Berneice Wilkinson

Thank you for your love, devotion,
and constant encouragement throughout
my life.

Contents

Foreword

"Or do you not know that your body is a temple of the Holy Spirit who is in you, whom you have from God, and that you are not your own? For you have been bought with a price: therefore glorify God in your body" (1 Corinthians 6:19, 20).

The Christian life is a supernatural life. It is not just a life which man lives through his own self-effort and self-imposed disciplines. In the Christian life, the living Christ walks around in human flesh and we become a suit of clothes for Him. All the fullness of the Godhead bodily is alive and indwelling us.

This supernatural quality of life must be demonstrated in such a way that others will see in us those attractive qualities of the Lord Jesus Christ. Today, as in no other time in history, Christians have opportunities to express their faith. The secular world is more open to the Christian witness than ever before. In *Harmony—How to Let God's Gifts Come Together in Your Life,* Diane Blacker has brought together the many and varied gifts which God has given us in order to enable us to live balanced and harmonious lives in Christ. She has emphasized certain facets which are often neglected, and has explained how such things as heredity, nutrition, and careful grooming are essential ingredients for the spiritual and physical life of every member of God's family.

As we observe the deterioration of so many standards, Christians as never before have the opportunity to exemplify high moral values, such as honesty, integrity, fulfilled marriages, and harmonious family life. Jesus Christ died to give us eternal life. In His Resurrection, we have the power to live in triumph over the problems of daily living.

God has given us every resource to live fully for Him. Many Christians are missing the joy of life because they neglect some of their most basic needs. *All* of life is important. Just as we need to seek spiritual nourishment from God's Word, we also need to learn how to give the proper care to our physical bodies—temples of the Holy Spirit. I have observed many times that individuals who, for various reasons—through eating the wrong food or taking the wrong drugs, whether or not prescribed— have developed a chemical imbalance and, as a result, are affected spiritually as well as physically, mentally, and emotionally. God has provided for *all* of our needs, and we need to utilize the gifts.

We are called to the high and holy calling of being able to glorify God and enjoy Him forever. In order to glorify Him we need to live lives of peace, joy, and love, as well as of fruitfulness and service. Our God-given, super-natural lives are attractive lives, which will inspire others to say, "I want that quality of life for myself."

Mrs. Blacker uses as her theme: "What you are is God's gift to you—what you make of yourself is your gift to God." You will enjoy reading *Harmony—How to Let God's Gifts Come Together in Your Life,* and your life will be greatly enriched in the process. A careful study of this book and application of the recommendations for letting God's gifts come together in our lives will help the reader to live a more balanced and harmonious life for Christ.

BILL BRIGHT

HARMONY

1
A Gift to God

WHAT YOU ARE IS GOD'S GIFT TO YOU . . .
WHAT YOU MAKE OF YOURSELF IS
YOUR GIFT TO GOD

A plaque bearing this inscription hangs on my kitchen wall. I have glanced at this saying hundreds of times, and reflected upon the significance of these words to us as Christians.

I think everyone delights in receiving a gift. I know I do—especially if it is given by someone who is very special to me. But I find as much pleasure in giving a gift as in receiving one. I want to show my affection or appreciation by choosing something specially suited for the one who is to be the recipient of the gift. A lot of time and thought goes into the giving of gifts between people who love one another.

When we think of receiving gifts from God, it is easy to count up all the blessings He has bestowed upon us. For example, my husband and I have three children whom we consider precious gifts from God. I have good health and talents which are gifts from Him. And He has blessed me most with the gift of new life in Jesus Christ. But somehow, it had never occurred to me that my life is my gift *to* God.

It's true; we are gifts *to* God. We have come into His family through faith in Jesus, to become His beloved children—precious and holy in His sight. In the same way parents adore and delight in their children, the Lord God delights in each of His children.

Early one sunny morning as I was sitting in the kitchen having a quiet time alone with the Lord, I suddenly became aware of the significance of the saying on our little plaque. My mind raced through the many im-

plications of the kind of gift I was giving God in my life.
Surely my Lord deserved the finest and best I had to
offer, yet the truth was that all too often He received only
the "leftovers" of my life. If I had time left over, I
prayed, read my Bible, or talked to the children about
Jesus. If I had time left over I could visit someone who
was ill or bake a fresh loaf of bread for a lonely friend.
Yes, there were a thousand things I could do to make the
gift of my life reflect the appreciation I had to God for
His gifts—if only I had enough time left over. Somehow
I was just so busy with other activities that I seldom had
time for the important things of life.

I'm so grateful that God still loves and accepts me,
even when I fall short of my best for Him. But now I
have been made aware of the fact that my life is a gift to
God. With this awareness has come a new desire and a
heightened sense of responsibility to give Him the best,
instead of the leftovers of my life.

Does God sometimes get just the leftovers of your life,
too? Would you like to give Him your best? If your answer is yes, will you consider with me, in the pages of
this book, how you can use the gifts God has given you to
make your life a treasured gift to Him?

Together we will explore some of the many gifts God
has given us. These heavenly gifts were given by a loving Father who desires each of His children to live in
harmony with one another. He has given us the ability
and the instruction to live well-balanced lives. In the
family of God we have the opportunity to live in security, with the confidence that He will provide for our
every need.

What You Are Is God's Gift to You

The gift of life is precious. But God has given us much
more than the breath of life. He created an entire universe, with mankind as the beneficiary of all His handi-
work.

We have been given eyes to see our world, ears to listen to its sounds, and the sense of smell to appreciate its fragrance. We have the ability to touch and feel with our hands and hearts. We have open, responsive minds to learn about life and its meaning. God's gifts extend far beyond the measure of our solitary lives.

Late one night as we were driving along the highway, I gazed out the window and was awed by the beauty of the starlit sky. I remember searching the darkness and trying to imagine how vast our universe is. What does it mean to have distance which knows no end? We measure everything, silly millimeters to light-years! Oh, how I longed to fathom the mind of God—to understand His creative ability in designing all the complexities of the universe, to comprehend the power of God in the creation and sustaining of all that He brought into existence. All of this was done for the purpose of giving life to mankind. We are the only part of God's creation with the ability to enjoy, ponder, and investigate the whole earth and part of what lies beyond it.

I particularly enjoy the springtime and planting seeds for flowers and vegetables. I am fascinated watching the tiny insects scurry about their business, working intently to acquire what they need for each day. It's the time of year when everything is coming alive after a long, cold winter—waking up and bursting with new life. But it is a life which will fade and be gone again in a few months.

In Jesus Christ, our Savior, we have life which never fades and never ends. True life—for everyone who will believe in Him. He is "the way, the truth, and the life" (John 14:6 KJV). We rejoice in this knowledge and are secure in this truth. However, we live in a world where God's truth is being rejected by people. Life is not precious for most of them; instead it has little meaning and much futility, even though a certain amount of knowledge and experience have been gained. As the Book of Ecclesiastes illustrates, life without God is not a treasured gift. It is simply vanity through the pursuit of knowledge. It is knowledge which is empty, because it lacks saving, redeeming grace.

What You Make of Yourself Is Your Gift to God

On the other hand, the Christian's purpose in life is completely different. God has designed a pattern for living that is available to every believer. The manner in which we handle this God-given life is our gift to God.

Personally, I want the days of my life to count for God's Kingdom. I want others to know how much I love Him. It is so good to be alive, and I am so happy God chose to give me life as a woman.

As a new Christian, unfamiliar with God's Word, I did not recognize my worth as a child of God. It has been exciting to discover Bible verses which describe how valuable we are in God's sight. The Book of Hebrews tells us we are members of the Royal Family, children of the King of Kings. We are chosen vessels of God, described in His Word as pure, holy, blameless, precious, temples of God, the dwelling place of His Holy Spirit. One day we shall all reside together in heaven. It is so marvelous that it is beyond our capacity to fully comprehend it!

It takes time to discover the riches which fill God's Word. It takes time to grow and mature in our Christian life. Yet sadly, most Christians seldom taste of life as God truly meant it to be. They only scratch the surface when it comes to experiencing what God offers us. There is an element of unbelief in us that is afraid to step out in faith, saying, "Here I am, Lord, show me, lead me, teach me how I can truly glorify You and be a banner of hope before my family and my neighborhood."

Banner of Hope

I believe the quality of life we exhibit to others is the banner we fly. We may wear symbols and emblems that say to others, "Look, I'm a Christian." But if our daily life isn't an example of what it means to be a Christian, our neighbors and friends will mock our Lord and call us hypocrites. It makes us cringe to think of it in this respect, doesn't it?

We live in an unbelieving world, yet a world searching for the meaning of life—a world that has every material luxury but seems to need more in order to be happy. People are escaping to cults, drugs, sex, and every other kind of perversion, trying to grasp something that will fill and satisfy their empty lives. We have what satisfies—only Jesus fills the empty void which is present in every heart. We need to fly this banner of hope for all to see.

I imagine we all have neighbors and co-workers whose lives are filled with heartaches and despair. Many of them are merely putting up a good front, making life appear satisfying outwardly. Perhaps you have lived that way too; I did. For years I functioned satisfactorily on the outside but was desperately unhappy on the inside.

I believe as Christians we have a responsibility to give an account of the hope that is in us. We need to exhibit in our daily lives a quality which says, "What I have will be good for you, too." If these people don't see Christ in us, who else will be able to show them the way?

Every area of our lives should reflect Christ and show the abundance of His love. I once heard a pastor say, "The thing you gaze on the most is what you will reflect." If we keep our eyes upon Jesus, then His attributes will be reflected through our lives. And this is a continuous, growing experience! In every one of our lives God is teaching, molding, and developing our characters.

We are continually being conformed into the image of our Lord Jesus. If there is one thing God continues to confirm in me, it is my need to stay close constantly to Him so He can guide and direct my way.

2

The Gift of God's Love to Me

I've had a lot of struggle in my life. I know that many of you have also come through some deep waters; others may be in them now.

When I first heard 1 Thessalonians 5:18, "In everything give thanks; for this is God's will for you in Christ Jesus," I did what God's Word said; I gave thanks. Yet, some of the circumstances in my life puzzled me; I didn't see why they were necessary. Surely life would have been less complicated and more enjoyable without them!

Now, years later, another verse has become my own precious promise: "Blessed be the God and Father of our Lord Jesus Christ, the Father of mercies and God of all comfort; who comforts us in all our affliction . . . with the comfort with which we ourselves are comforted by God" (2 Corinthians 1:3, 4).

After I began a ministry of speaking and teaching, I realized why some of the trials were necessary. Without trials, how can I possibly have an understanding of what others are going through? Now I can honestly give thanks with the confidence that no trial or difficulty was in vain.

It Wasn't Always This Way

Confidence and security in Christ were not a part of my early life, for I have only known Jesus as my Savior since 1964. Years of quiet desperation and insecurity preceded my new birth and are still fresh in my mind.

As a child, I spent hours daydreaming. It was an escape from the loneliness and unhappiness I felt. In the world of make-believe, you can be everything you're really not.

My parents were divorced when I was very young, and

my dear mother had to go to work. My brother is three years older than I, and though we were very close, I spent a great deal of time alone.

I was given all the lessons to prepare for the career I dreamed about and also given the responsibility to attend the classes. As a child of ten I could ride the bus or streetcar all over the city of Minneapolis, depending on where I was going for which lesson! I began taking dancing lessons at two years of age, skating lessons at four, and elocution and piano came shortly thereafter.

The summer before I began high school, Mother was offered a position in Beverly Hills, California, so Mom and I headed west. What an adventure for the two of us! We bought a shiny red Pontiac convertible, and had a great time discovering the big city of Los Angeles. In short order, we found an apartment in Westwood and an ice rink in Pasadena. After a few months of commuting from Westwood to Pasadena to skate, someone asked me why I didn't skate at the rink in Hollywood, which was only half the distance.

The following summer, while skating at the Hollywood rink, I collided—literally—with the neatest, nicest boy I had ever met! His name was Mike Blacker, and he had just arrived on the train from Champaign, Illinois, with eight dollars, his skates, and his suitcase in hand. He had just been hired at the rink.

We talked the entire evening. It was my night to practice, but I never put on my skates. He told me all about himself—terrific lines which impressed me at the time but didn't turn out to be too accurate!

My mother claims I came home and said, "Well, I've met him—the one I'm going to marry!" To me he was everything a girl could ever hope for—polite, clean-cut, ambitious, and hardworking, with emphasis on the latter—he had four jobs!

Monday became our regular date night. I would go to the rink to skate after school and we would take the bus to my house. I usually cooked dinner, and sometime between "I Love Lucy" and "Gunsmoke," Mike would fall asleep, exhausted from all those jobs! Every Monday night, Mom and I would wake him about eleven o'clock, just in time to catch the last bus home.

We soon began to talk about getting married someday, and we decided that if Mike were going to support us in the manner to which we wished to become accustomed, he really ought to go to college! Soon he went back to Illinois, and for the next two years we went steady by correspondence. I finished high school while Mike worked and attended college.

By the end of high school, the career I had dreamed about looked even more enticing. Mike's number had come up for the military; he joined the air force. So when the Ice Follies came to town, I decided to audition. I joined the show, along with some of my childhood friends from Minneapolis and two friends from Los Angeles.

We skated in twenty-five major cities in the United States and Canada, performing before tens of thousands of people a year. My costumes often cost as much as two thousand dollars apiece. I did many television shows for publicity, and loved it!

Mike and I decided to elope when I had two days off between the Denver and Chicago shows. He was going into pilot training in the air force and we thought it would be easier being married and apart rather than just apart. We found a pastor unpacking his suitcase in his first pastorate, a small Presbyterian church. We were the first couple he had ever married. His wife played the piano, his little girl cried, and I cried, too.

I was thrilled to be married, but sad that it had to be kept a secret. Mother had talked often about the beautiful wedding dress and veil she would make for me one day. As I looked down at my beige tweed, I couldn't help but feel a twinge of sadness because she wasn't there to share this moment. Indeed, she didn't even know until many months later that we were married. (I have often prayed that none of our children will deny us the joy of seeing them united in marriage to their beloved.)

After the ceremony, we drove to Chicago, the show opened, and I skated on our wedding night!

Being married but apart was not as easy as we had thought it would be. During our first two and one half years of marriage, we spent only ninety days together. We had gone steady by correspondence; now we were married and still writing scores of letters!

While I skated and waited, I diligently saved my money for a car and the down payment on a trailer. Mike's parents, Jim and Carolyn Blacker, helped us accumulate a few household possessions.

Soda Crackers and Furry Critters

When Mike was commissioned a second lieutenant, his parents and I drove to Texas to watch the ceremony. I pinned the pilot wings on him. Our future looked wonderful. I had left the Ice Follies permanently, and no two people have ever been happier about finally being together.

Our little home on wheels was like a palace to us, just because we were together. We hoped for a baby right away, and before long our number-one daughter was on the way. I was so thrilled and proud to be "expecting." We were sure this was our greatest accomplishment!

We were based in Texas, where Mike was going through advanced flying school. It seemed to me he was flying day and night *eight* days a week! It wasn't long before I realized the honeymoon was over. I sat alone, pregnant, and so nauseated that for weeks the only two foods I could keep down were soda crackers and cream of mushroom soup. Mice were somehow invading our little palace and, frankly, I have never had much affection for the furry little critters. If this wasn't enough, it was 115 degrees in the bright Texas sun. Each night when Mike came home, he'd empty and reset the mousetraps, and tell me about all the wonderful experiences he had had that day. In the fall, we were transferred to Shaw Air Force Base in Sumter, South Carolina, so Mike could take additional advanced flight training.

We have fond memories of Sumter, especially because our first daughter, Cindy, was born there. She surprised us by coming a month early after only an hour and twenty minutes of labor! We thought we were prepared to be parents, but we had planned to buy all the necessary equipment during the coming month. Mike had to dash out and get everything in one day! He fixed up the little nursery in the trailer and three days later we brought Cindy home from the hospital.

We bought our first home a few months later and it was fun furnishing it with early "cast offs" from our parents and the local secondhand store. We were only in the house a few months when orders came for both the 17th and 18th Tactical Reconnaissance Squadrons to move to France. Each of the pilots flew their RF 101s across the Atlantic Ocean. The wives and children followed four months later.

Mike welcomed us to France and our new home—an eight-by-thirty-five-foot trailer. Practically the first words he spoke were, "Guess what they have right here on the base? A University of Maryland Extension. I can take college-credit courses toward my bachelor's degree."

Babies and Bridge

And it began—Mike flew in the squadron by day and went to school at night for the duration of our three-and-a-half-year tour in France. I spent most of my time playing bridge with the gals in the neighborhood. There was always a game in progress somewhere. When our husbands were on alert and had to stay in the squadron building, or when they would go to Morocco to fly for a few days, we would play bridge twelve or fourteen hours a day.

My life didn't consist of an endless game of bridge, though. In February 1962, our second daughter, Susan, was born. When we told Cindy about the new baby we were expecting she immediately replied, "Oh, goodie, God is going to send me a baby sister and her name will be Susan Diane!" We never considered the possibility of a boy and of course dared not choose another name! The girls have been a tremendous source of joy in my life.

One Degree Down, One to Go

Mike had gone to school four nights a week during our tour in France. When we came back to the States, he attended the University of Nebraska at Omaha for a semester of on-campus study which was necessary to receive his degree. In March 1964—twelve years after he decided to go to college—Mike finally received that prized diploma.

After Omaha, Mike was transferred to Maxwell Air Force Base, his first assignment choice. Guess why? There is a night law school in Montgomery! The day he checked into the base, he also began night classes toward a law degree. That hardworking dedication I had admired so much so long ago was beginning to really get to me!

Hollow Foundation

Outwardly, I encouraged Mike in his educational pursuits. I wanted him to attain his goals. He worked hard and studied hard. He went to school four nights a week for seven years while he was an air-force pilot, to earn his bachelor of arts and bachelor of law degrees.

Inwardly, I was devastated. After ten years of marriage, I was a desperately lonely and resentful young woman. All my life I had longed for companionship and time with the ones I love. I felt I had never had this.

I had searched for God, but He had remained hidden from me. Mike and I seldom had time alone together. We had no real communication, no common goals for our marriage or the raising of our family. We had no friendships with other couples, no hobbies or mutual interests.

How can one be surrounded with activity, meeting the constant needs of three other people and still feel completely alone? I was sure no one else would understand my feelings, so I never talked about them with anyone.

Southern Hospitality

The house we purchased in Montgomery was owned by a lady named Mickey Smith. One of the first things she asked me was, "What church do you go to?" I replied, "Presbyterian." After all, we had eloped to a Presbyterian church, so I figured that was enough to make me a Presbyterian!

"Good," she replied, "so do I. I'll take you to church with me Sunday." I didn't want to embarrass myself by refusing, and I couldn't think of a good excuse not to go, so I gulped something profound like, "Oh—ah, okay!"

I had attended Sunday school and church as a youngster. I attended churches all over the country when I skated. We went to chapel frequently while we were in France, too. Cindy had rarely missed Sunday school in the past three years, and both girls had been baptized as infants.

For years I had yearned to know God, but I had never heard that He was interested in me. There were times when I wept, crying out to God, "Oh, God, if You exist, won't You help me? I am so miserable." But now I hadn't been to church for more than a year, because I had given up hope that I would ever find an answer to the meaning of life.

All these years I was functioning outwardly very well. I knew how to be well groomed, I kept a clean house, cooked good meals, cared for the girls, made all our clothes, did nice things for people—all the "right" things to do. But that was on the outside—on the inside, I felt sheer desperation!

Well, Cindy, Susan, and I attended Sunday school with my new friend. To be honest, I didn't understand a thing they were talking about. When we returned home I told Mike that I was going back, because I felt in the class I could find the answers I had sought for so long.

I presume, by virtue of the fact that I attended the class, everyone thought I was a Christian. I was not going to show my ignorance by asking questions about all those big words they were using. You know the words—justification, sanctification, propitiation. I just figured if I sat there long enough I'd absorb whatever they had that made them so different. I could see the difference on their faces and in a quality of life they possessed which I did not have. They talked about having a meaningful, abundant life and that's what I wanted, because there surely wasn't anything abundant about my life.

One evening about three weeks later the pastor, our dearly loved Dr. Robert Strong, came to call. It was a pleasant though slightly awkward time, but the next week Mike attended church with us. In May we joined the church. There were three ways you could become a member: transfer of letter, profession of faith, or reaffirmation of faith. Mike chose transfer of letter, because he had been baptized by immersion at a church when he was eleven. (All his friends had joined there because they had a gymnasium and roller skating.) I chose to join on profession of faith; I had no letter and nothing to reaffirm!

Shortly after I first attended the Sunday-school class a survey of the Bible was begun. We studied one or more books a week, so that in a few months we actually went through the entire Bible. I thought, "Wow, here's my chance to find the answers." Mike had purchased a King James Version of the Bible when we set up housekeeping saying, "Every home should have one." I eagerly took it off the shelf and began to read—Genesis, Exodus, Leviticus, and so on through the Bible. I really got hung up in the thees and thous and begats, but I kept on reading. Finally, forty-four books later, the study group and I came to the Book of Romans. Our teacher said, "There is a new book called Living Letters which is a paraphrase of the Epistles. I think you would enjoy reading this easy-to-understand style."

I couldn't buy it fast enough! As I read, it all became so clear. "Now God says he will accept and acquit us— declare us 'not guilty'—if we trust Jesus Christ to take away our sins. And we all can be saved in this way, by coming to Christ, no matter who we are or what we have been like" (Romans 3:22 LB). For the first time, I realized I was included, and I said aloud, "That's me, Lord Jesus, You died for me!" Suddenly He was not just *the* Savior—He was *my* Savior, and I knew it for certain!

I was so excited! I really wasn't alone after all! He was with me!

I read on, devouring every page. Then I came to Romans 12:2, where Paul says, "Don't copy the behavior and customs of this world, but be a new and different person with a fresh newness in all you do and think. Then you will learn from your own experience how his ways will really satisfy you" (LB). *Now* I had hope.

Do You Have Hope?

Perhaps some of you identify with the way I felt, shattered on the inside even when you are intact on the outside. Who puts you back together again when you feel this way? Who gives you self-control when you have lost patience with your children? Who gives you love for your mate or others in the family or on your job when they don't respond to your efforts? Those are things I can't give. I couldn't even give them to myself, but God can—free of charge.

Have you given your heart to Jesus, asking Him to be your Savior? Or could it be that, if you are already a Christian, you have been holding back from God—afraid to trust Him with the problems in your life? Do you sometimes feel the pressures are too heavy to carry alone?

Often we forget that God actually cares more for us than we do for ourselves. He is interested in every concern of our lives. He also knows that there is a more abundant life for us if we will give Him the opportunity to show us His greatness.

God offers us a fresh, new start with only one condition: we must be cleansed and free from sin in our lives. We simply cannot work our way to heaven no matter how earnestly we try, nor can we remove our own sin. God, in His love, provided the payment for our sins when our precious Lord Jesus came down from heaven, was born as a baby, and lived a perfect and sinless life in order to be the pure, holy sacrifice which was necessary to cover the sins of all who came after Him. He went to the cross willingly, bearing all of our sins on His own body, and suffered there the agony of separation from God, so we could be freed from the penalty and guilt our sin brings upon us.

For many years, *sin* was a foreign word to me. Oh, I knew the word. It just didn't seem to apply to my life. When you think of the word *sin*, what comes to mind? I always thought of things such as murder, stealing, wild, riotous living, some of what the kids today call the "gross things." But the Bible includes other things which really surprised me: worry, discouragement, gossip, unbelief, pride. These sins are not only actions but attitudes as well. The Bible often describes sin as an attitude, our attitude toward God and how much we are willing or unwilling to involve Him in our daily lives.

God gives us a wonderful promise in 1 John 1:9: "If we confess our sins, he [God] is faithful and just to forgive us our sins, and to cleanse us from all unrighteousness" (KJV)—a clean slate, making it possible to receive and appropriate His gift of power and new life in Jesus Christ. Jesus is our only hope, the only way we can come to God. In the Gospel of John 14:6, Jesus said, "I am the way, and the truth, and the life; no one comes to the Father, but through Me."

Coming to Jesus is a step of faith so simple, according to the Scriptures, that even children can understand. Acts 16:31 says, "Believe in the Lord Jesus, and you shall be saved . . . ." Romans 10:9, 10 tells how to go about it: "If you confess with your mouth Jesus as Lord, and believe in your heart that God raised Him from the dead, you shall be saved; for with the heart man believes, resulting in righteousness, and with the mouth he confesses, resulting in salvation."

If you have never come to Christ in faith, believing and confessing Him as your Savior and Lord, won't you do it today? Come into the love and fellowship of God's family. All that Jesus has by God's authority will be yours.

Prayer is an attitude of the heart and mind. God is not nearly as concerned with the words you say as He is with the attitude of your heart. A simple prayer such as this one, offered from a sincere and open heart, is enough to come into trusting faith in Him: "Dear Jesus, I know that I am a sinner who needs You as my Savior. Please come into my life, forgive my sin, and make me the kind of person You want me to be. Thank You for loving me, and for Your promise to give me life everlasting. Amen."

No experience or achievement in life is of any significance when compared to knowing Christ. Whether male or female, we share many of the same hopes and dreams, the same needs and desires. Regardless of our background, the only true fulfillment for us in our world today is found in the person of Jesus Christ. He has absolutely everything we need. He has the power to enable us to live *above* our circumstances. His perfect love gives us the desire and ability to face each day with joy and anticipation, wondering how He will work through us to convey His love to others.

3

Living in Harmony With Jesus

When the promises and power of God are available to us, why do so many Christians continue to live in spiritual poverty? Many spend years as bitter, resentful, angry, frustrated people.

It is easy to understand these kinds of attitudes in non-Christians, but I am speaking now of Christians. Many Christians live with these negative attitudes dominating their lives. With the power available to us, it simply should not be this way.

After I received God's gift of everlasting life in Jesus, I seemed to live on a roller coaster with more down times than up. I didn't know that an abundant life was available to me *every* day. The abundant life means being peaceful, secure, and confident on the inside, even when circumstances on the outside are not exactly the way we wish they were.

I understand now how my attitude in *certain* areas of my life affects *every* area of it. If I am bitter in one area, other areas are affected by my bitterness as well.

How Should We Respond to God?

God knows me completely; there is nothing in my being which I can hide from Him. He also knows what I am capable of becoming if I will allow Him to guide and instruct me.

God doesn't love us and then leave us to our own devices, to wonder and worry about what the future may hold. On the contrary, He loves and guides us in the Christian life, so that it becomes a growing experience which continues until the day we are taken home to be with Him.

It is a sad thing when a child is born into a family and

remains an infant in mind or body. The same is true of a believer who is born into God's family, but remains a baby in Christ, never developing or growing into the mature person he is meant to become (*see* 1 Peter 2:2).

All of God's resources are available to us to aid us in becoming mature, well-balanced Christians. But there is one basic requirement—a willing spirit. The willing spirit comes to God saying, "Here I am, Lord; teach me, use me in whatever way I can best glorify You. I want others to see Jesus in me and I know this is only possible when He is in control of my life. Cleanse me from all unrighteousness, I pray, and fill me with the power of Your Holy Spirit."

God wants us to live consistent lives, well balanced and in harmony with the principles found in Scripture. As fallen beings, we lack the capacity to live a God-centered life in our own power.

I had been an eager, growing Christian in the three years since my conversion. I had been president of our Sunday-school class and was teaching an adult group on a regular basis. I had spent hours delving into commentaries on Scripture, had read my Bible through several times, and loved the fellowship of my church. However, I couldn't understand why I had high times and low times instead of the consistency I felt should be more in keeping with one's Christian life.

During the summer of 1967 our church sponsored a Lay Institute for Evangelism, conducted by staff of the Lay Ministry of Campus Crusade for Christ. It was there that I heard the simple explanation of the difference between a Christ-controlled life and a self-controlled life. I immediately recognized that there lay the reason for the imbalance in my life. I was simply ignorant of the ministry of the Holy Spirit in my life. I wanted all the benefits of a godly life, but lacked the knowledge of how to appropriate what was available to me in Christ.

I appreciate someone who can give me a "how to" I

can really grasp. Campus Crusade did that with their booklet *Have You Made the Wonderful Discovery of the Spirit-Filled Life?* The diagrams in this booklet are easy to understand; the message is clear. It was used by God to deepen my Christian commitment and I highly recommend it.

This booklet is available at Christian bookstores or by writing to Campus Crusade for Christ International, Arrowhead Springs, San Bernardino, California 92404. The basic message is this: The Bible tells us there are three kinds of people—the natural man, who has not received Christ (*see* 1 Corinthians 2:14); the spiritual man, who is a Spirit-controlled Christian (*see* 1 Corinthians 2:15); and the carnal man, who professes Christ but is trying to control his life himself (*see* 1 Corinthians 3:1–3).

It is interesting how often a carnal Christian's life can resemble the life of the non-Christian. Whenever a person is trying to control his own life and destiny there will be discord and a certain amount of frustration and anxiety.

On the other hand, every day can be an exciting day for the Christian who knows the reality of being filled with the Holy Spirit and who lives constantly, moment by moment, under His gracious control.

All the resources of God are available to the Christian to live an abundant and fruitful Christian life (*see* John 10:10, 15:5; Galatians 5:22, 23; Acts 1:8). When you yield the control of your life to Jesus by surrendering your self-will to His will, then you can be assured that God will fill you and empower you with His Holy Spirit. You will know the reality of His power as you begin to experience it daily in your life. The evidence will come in the form of personal traits and Christlike characteristics: your life and thoughts will be Christ centered and empowered by the Holy Spirit; you will be able to speak more freely with your friends about Jesus and introduce them to Him; understanding of God's Word will increase and your prayer life will become more effective. You will begin to have greater trust in God and desire to be more obedient to what the Scripture teaches concerning Christian living. As you grow in faith and maturity these characteristics will increase. Obviously one who is just beginning to understand all that is available in Christ will not exhibit or experience the same depth of quality as the person who yielded the control of his life to Christ many years before.

For a variety of reasons, most Christians are not experiencing the abundant life. If a person is carnal and is trusting in his own efforts instead of God for each day's need, his fellowship with God is broken. Often he is simply ignorant of his spiritual heritage, just as I was. He may have lost his first love for God and others, or have doubts about God's sufficiency because he is not studying the Word or having a meaningful prayer life. Often his life reflects discouragement, resentment, guilt, a critical spirit, impure thoughts, or a very legalistic attitude (*see* Romans 5:8–10; Hebrews 10:1–25; 1 John 1, 2:1–3; 2 Peter 1:9; Acts 1:8).

We become Christians through the ministry of the Holy Spirit (*see* John 3:1–8), and from the moment of spiritual birth every Christian is indwelt by the Holy Spirit at all times (*see* John 1:12; Colossians 2:9, 10; John 14:16, 17). Even though all Christians are indwelt by the Holy Spirit, not all Christians are filled (controlled and empowered) by the Holy Spirit (*see* John 7:37–39, 16:1–15; Acts 1:1–9). We are filled (controlled and empowered) by the Holy Spirit by faith; then we can know and experience the abundant and fruitful Christian life.

This is the life I wanted and to learn that it was a step of faith was good news indeed. As I read this message, I realized the qualities called the "fruit of the Spirit" listed in Galatians 5:22, 23 are simply the attitudes and attributes of Jesus. These attitudes are available to us in exchange for the old negative attitudes which keep us bogged down and feeling defeated. What a fantastic swap!

One day, as an act of my faith, I gave Jesus my anxieties, resentments, and my nagging, critical spirit. In return—not all at once, but slowly, as I was able to deal with them—He gave me some of the fruit of the Spirit; new love for others, a sense of joy and peace, and a sprinkling of patience and kindness.

But greatest of all, God gave me the faith to trust Him to keep all those ugly attitudes out of my life. That didn't make me a puppet either; it made me free. It gave me freedom to grow and to realize the full potential available to me as a Christian. This is not life's second best, but the *very best* from the only One who can make it a reality—God Almighty, the giver of life.

There is nothing complicated about being a Spirit-filled-and-controlled Christian. It is a step of faith which is made in the complete confidence that God is true to His promises. (Please notice I did not say it was *easy* to live the Spirit-filled life—it is just *uncomplicated* to appropriate it.)

I learned that I must trust God in a "moment by moment" relationship. When I sinned I needed to confess it immediately and thank God for bringing it to my attention and for changing the direction of my life. I can't harbor or hang onto wrong attitudes or actions once I have been made aware of them. I must give them to Jesus and trust Him to handle them and continue to live and love through me. Jesus always keeps His promises. No matter what happens in our lives the Holy Spirit is always present and is our continual source of power and strength.

One Man's Search for Harmony

I wanted to share with Mike all the things I was experiencing in Christ, but I realized that even though he attended church with us, he had not made a completely dedicated personal commitment. He was very happy that I was active in the church, and he enjoyed the fellowship, too. It gave us another very nice outward appearance, but my inner needs for companionship and communication with my husband were still not being met.

I was learning to trust God in all circumstances of my life. I was beginning to realize that problems should be viewed as opportunities to trust God more fully and see what He will do through a yielded life. So, as I was learning to continually draw closer to God, in complete dependence for each day's need, I entrusted my personal needs where Mike was concerned to the Father.

One evening, seven years after my conversion, Mike asked me if I thought he was a Christian. I explained that no one can know for certain about another person's relationship to Jesus, but that God promises to change our lives when we come to Christ in faith and receive Him as our Savior. I told him honestly that, as far as I could see, there was no evidence of change in his life.

Several months later, Mike questioned a friend about some cassette tapes he was carrying. The friend explained that they were tapes put out by Campus Crusade staff members who spoke on college campuses around the country.

Mike borrowed the tapes and, for the next six weeks, had his cassette recorder with him constantly, listening to the tapes over and over again. Frequently he'd play a portion for me and exclaim, "Hey, listen to this! Have you ever heard that before?"

I'd reply, "Yes, honey, isn't that wonderful!" He just couldn't seem to get enough of those messages!

My mother was planning to move to Montgomery, and Mike had flown to California to drive her car back for her. By coincidence a weekend seminar was being led at Campus Crusade's headquarters in Arrowhead Springs, California.

On impulse, Mike decided to check out the place where all those tapes had come from. An Alabama staff member greeted him warmly, and Mike decided to stay for the next seminar, which was a workshop on how to use the *Four Spiritual Laws* booklet.

A message about developing one's personal relationship with Jesus followed the seminar. At the close of this message, each person was asked to find a quiet place where he could feel alone with God. During this time, each person was to ask God to bring to his remembrance all sins which remained in his life—sins which had not been repented of or confessed.

Mike chose a spot overlooking the city. He began listing things which were wrong in his life and soon realized he had never confessed *anything* before. In fact, he realized he had never really prayed and, in truth, didn't have a relationship with Jesus at all.

On the side of that mountain overlooking the city lights, Mike prayed to receive Christ.

It was after 1:30 A.M. in Montgomery when I was awakened by the ringing telephone, but believe me, it was worth the loss of sleep to hear Mike ask if we could pray together! It was the first time in seventeen years of marriage that we had ever prayed together, and one of the most precious moments of my life.

Mike devoured Bible-study materials, and we soon joined the staff of Campus Crusade, working as associate members of the Lay Ministry in Montgomery. Mike continued to practice law, but the change I had prayed for had occurred. He began to lead many of his clients to Jesus.

4

The Fullness of God

Have you ever wondered what God is really like, and what it will be like to experience heaven and see Jesus face to face?

Can you imagine the greatness of a Being who has the ability to create each of the plant and animal species with all of their delicate parts and inner workings?

Imagine it! We Christians personally know and communicate with the God of the universe who knows *everything* about *everything!* I don't know about you—but that boggles my mind! I want to increasingly experience the fullness of God in my life and I believe this is the basic desire of most Christians.

The Bible tells us we are born into God's family through our faith in Jesus Christ. Our natural family is still an important part of our heritage, but now we have gained a new Father and a new family. With this new spiritual birth comes the birthright and inheritance which belongs to every child of God.

What we inherit from our earthly family is evident. We inherit physical features and intellect. Our parents were responsible for our home environment, education, and monetary benefits.

But our new inheritance as a child of God far surpasses anything our earthly parents could supply. With God, we are not limited to our own human resources. Through God, we have resources beyond our knowledge and experience, beyond our comprehension.

It has been said that Albert Einstein had 1 percent of total knowledge. I imagine most of us would agree he was a mental genius. If he actually knew 1 percent of all things, just try to imagine how much there is for you and me to learn! And this is particularly true in my knowledge of God. However, the more I study the Bible, the more I discover how much of Him has been revealed there. In fact, everything God wants us to know about Himself has been recorded in the Bible. We know Him through what we read, as the Holy Spirit illumines our minds, and we know Him as we experience the reality of our relationship with Him in our everyday lives.

Scholars have spent their entire lives pondering, studying, and researching the subject of our Creator. The more I read what has been written about the attributes of God, the more thankful I am that we accept Him by faith and not by knowledge. Our faith is based on facts which are logical, all inclusive, and true; but *faith* is the important ingredient when a finite created being is seeking to know and understand the Infinite Creator.

Who Is God?

For the gifts and the calling of God are irrevocable . . . . Oh, the depth of the riches both of the wisdom and knowledge of God! How unsearchable are His judgments and unfathomable His ways! For who has known the mind of the Lord, or who became His counselor? Or who has first given to Him that it might be paid back to Him again? For from Him and through Him and to Him are all things. To Him be the glory forever. Amen.

Romans 11:29, 33–36

The Bible tells us many things about God. He is a Spirit—omnipotent (all powerful), omniscient (all knowing), and omnipresent (everywhere). He has always existed and is unchangeable in His being and attributes.

In the *Westminster Confession of Faith*, He is described as:

. . . an infinite being, perfect, a most pure Spirit, invisible, without body parts or passions, immutable, immense, eternal, Almighty, most wise, most holy, most free, most absolute, righteous, loving, gracious, merciful, long-suffering, abundant in truth. He is just, hates all sin and will hold accountable for sin those who are guilty. He has all life, glory, goodness, blessedness and is all-sufficient, sovereign and infallible.

Undoubtedly, other qualities could be added to this list; yet, it is enough to make us stand back in awe. And our God, in His majesty and greatness, cares for each one of us! Even the least significant aspect of our being is of importance to Him. How can we help but respond in reverence and thankfulness to God when the reality of His acceptance of us becomes real to us?

It is important that we do not fall into the trap of putting more emphasis on one attribute than another. God *is*—He is not more loving than He is just, merciful, holy, immense, eternal, or incomprehensible. He is all that He is—totally.

I think more people are drawn to God because of the love He has for us than because of their fear of the judgment which awaits those who reject Him. If asked, "To you, what is the greatest attribute of God?" most Christians would unhesitatingly reply, "His love."

God's Love Is Evident

Because of God's love, we have the written Word. Had God not loved us and had concern for His special creation, He would not have made it possible for us to come to Him and know Him. Nature and creation point to the source, the Creator. Scripture attests to the abiding love, care, and concern of the Creator for His creation.

I thank God that we do not have to depend on what others imagined God to be (*see* 1 Thessalonians 2:13). We can rely completely upon God Himself because He has revealed Himself to us through the Holy Scriptures.

God Triune

The Bible states clearly that there is but one God, manifest in three persons—the Father, the Son, and the Holy Spirit. These three are the one, true, eternal God—the same in substance, equal in power and glory, although distinguished by their primary function.

The Scriptures declare that Jesus and the Holy Spirit are God—equal with the Father, giving them the common names, characteristics, works, and worship as are proper only to God.

Although the Bible does not use the word *trinity* to describe the Godhead, Scripture references demonstrating the common characteristics of this three-in-one God are plentiful (*see* Isaiah 9:6; Jeremiah 23:6; Matthew 3:16, 17, 28:19; John 1:1, 4, 2:24, 25, 15:26; Acts 5:3, 4; 2 Corinthians 13:14; Galatians 4:6; Colossians 1:16; Hebrews 1:5, 9:14).

I realize these statements are complex. I feel, though, that it is necessary to have an accurate picture of God. If I look at God as some kind of "Big Daddy" figure, I will respond to Him the way I picture Him. But if I have an accurate picture of who God has declared Himself to be in holiness, majesty, and power, as well as in love and mercy, I will then respond to Him in a fitting and proper way.

Learning About Scripture

Bible study is essential for every believer. Within the pages of the Bible is written for us everything we *need* to know about God and the life we are to live as Christians. Only through study can we learn about God and the inheritance we possess as His children.

A good verse to memorize is 2 Timothy 3:16, 17: "All Scripture is inspired by God and profitable for teaching, for reproof, for correction, for training in righteousness; that the man of God may be adequate, equipped for every good work."

"Inspired" in the Greek literally means "God breathed." The Bible is not just a collection of books about the history of a nation and people, or comfortable rules which may or may not be applied to one's life. The Scriptures were God breathed into the minds of the human writers God chose to convey His message. They wrote the very words given to them by Almighty God. Nothing was written without purpose or without specific intent for the generations to come. The Bible is as applicable to us today as it has been to all other generations in history. Second Timothy 3:16, 17 is more than a statement; it is a promise, an unshakable truth.

For centuries, men have tried to destroy the credibility of the Scriptures. They have sought to distort its teachings, add to what it says, or take away from what it states. But the *truth* of God's Word stands firm. God, through the power of His Holy Spirit, confirms truth in the hearts and minds of His own children. Every true believer in Jesus Christ can attest to that fact.

The Apostle Paul, in his letter to the Romans, states in chapter 8, verse 16: "The Spirit Himself bears witness with our spirit that we are children of God."

The Apostle John also confirms this truth in his epistle, 1 John 5:10–15 (author's italics):

The one who believes in the Son of God has the witness in himself; the one who does not believe God has made Him a liar, because he has not believed in the witness that God has borne concerning His Son. And the witness is this, that God has given us eternal life, and this life is in His Son. He who has the Son has the life; he who does not have the Son of God does not have the life. *These things I have written to you who believe in the name of the Son of God, in order that you may know that you have eternal life.* And this is the confidence which we have before Him, that, if we ask anything according to His will, He hears us. And if we know that He hears us in whatever we ask, we know that we have the requests which we have asked from Him.

Much of our personal growth and maturity in the Christian life will come through diligent, devoted study of the Scriptures.

It is a great blessing to be a member of a church where Christ is honored and the Word of God is preached in truth. And it is a blessing to have the fellowship of other Christians in a Bible study. But neither of these should be a substitute for the time we spend in personal Bible study.

God does not want His children to remain on the kindergarten level of spiritual growth. We are to grow up in Christ (*see* Ephesians 4:14, 15), increasing our knowledge and understanding of His Word. Only in this way can we derive the benefits for living which are part of our inheritance in the family of God. Truly, the fullness and depth of our life in Christ comes through the hours we give to prayer and study.

The Accurate Division

"Study *and* be eager *and* do your utmost to present yourself to God approved (tested by trial), a workman who has no cause to be ashamed, correctly analyzing *and* accurately dividing—rightly handling and skillfully teaching—the Word of Truth" (2 Timothy 2:15 AMPLIFIED).

As we study to increase our understanding of the Scriptures, we want to be sure we are, in so far as we can see, correctly interpreting what the Bible says. There are two types of interpretations which we should use—literal and contextual. The Word of God is clear and can be understood by the layman. Literal interpreters look at the naturally accepted meaning of terms. In other words, we can believe that the person speaking meant what he said, even when he used figures of speech or analogies to communicate his message.

We should be aware of the danger involved in "spiritualization," however. This is taking a word out of context and using it to support our own particular argument. For instance, let's say I have been asked to give a devotional at a meeting and I have been given a particular subject on which to speak. I think, "Wow, that's not going to be easy!" And I rush to my Bible, looking for a single verse which will hopefully substantiate my subject. Suddenly I find just the right verse, but when I read the whole chapter I find that the context from which it comes bears no resemblance to my assigned theme. Now I am faced with the big decision—to lift or not to lift out of context.

Contextual Interpretation

Doctor Earl D. Radmacher, president of Western Baptist Conservative Seminary, taught me a good way to remember the correct use of the Word of God. He has a saying, "Every text has a context and a text taken out of its context is a pretext . . . it is not *truth*." One can see here the importance of reading whole chapters and books, and of taking the time to use a good commentary in order to familiarize oneself with the historical background of the time.

How to Study the Bible

I have found seven principles to be of particular help to me in my Bible study. It is helpful to me to keep a prayer calendar or notebook handy for recording insights gained from my reading or to record questions which come to my mind.

We should begin our special study times with the prayer that the Holy Spirit will give us understanding of what we read.

1. Study systematically: I have found it more enlightening to study full chapters or entire books at one

sitting. This way, I get the contextual meaning as well as the literal meaning.

2. Study regularly: Sometimes it is difficult to make time, but Bible study must come high on our priority list if we are to continue to mature in the Christian life.

3. Study with variety: I enjoy using more than one translation. Each can give us different insights, especially when used interchangeably.

4. Study alertly: I suppose this is why so many people prefer the morning for their personal devotions. They are awake! Half the time we read and pray just as we are going to sleep. Often I am tempted to say "Amen" when I wake up in the morning because I didn't finish my prayer the night before!

5. Study prayerfully: I ask the Holy Spirit to illuminate my heart and mind, to give me understanding and the ability to apply wisely His Word to my life.

6. Study expectantly: I expect God to give me something to live by that day. And He gives me just what I need!

7. Study obediently: I think this is of particular importance, because God speaks to us through His Word. When you are reading the Bible, you may come to a point where God will impress upon your mind clearly, "I want you to do this . . . ." If you fail to obey, that's when your fellowship with God is hindered. Don't miss the blessing that comes through obedience.

5

The Gift of Prayer

You will guard him *and* keep him in perfect *and* constant peace whose mind [both its inclination and its character] is stayed on You, because he commits himself to You, leans on You *and* hopes confidently in You.

Isaiah 26:3 AMPLIFIED

Nothing seems to play a greater role in our growth and maturity as Christians than developing the right attitudes by centering our thoughts upon Jesus. When our first priority is to be the person He wants us to be, we will live in conscious recognition of His abiding presence.

We will weigh our actions and reactions, desiring to glorify Him through them. Unfortunately, we will never attain perfection in these areas on this earth and we must not allow ourselves to become discouraged when we fall short. We must confess the problem and, being grateful for God's forgiveness, just keep on keeping on.

The Quiet Time

Maintaining a regular time alone with God for prayer and Scripture reading is one of the best ways to keep a healthy attitude and perspective about life. We grow in confidence and maturity through this quiet, daily fellowship with Him.

Thinking about the need for time with God and planning to do it sometime in the future isn't good enough. I know; I've been that route, and my spiritual life stagnated.

Scripture does not say, "Pray if you feel like it." We

read in 1 Thessalonians 5:17, "Pray without ceasing." I pray everywhere I go, but I also have a *planned* quiet time. I have found the early morning to be the best time for me. The house is quiet; others are still asleep. It is a priceless time to me, preparation for the whole day.

You may find other times of the day or evening more suitable for your needs. Certainly quiet times are not limited to any one hour of the day. The important thing is that you *make* the time.

Prayer the ACTS Way

Prayer for the Christian should be a time of rich fellowship with our heavenly Father. If you have recently become a Christian or have never established a prayer time before, you may benefit from some suggestions on how to pray.

In my book *Totally New*, Guidelines for New Christians, I wrote a brief chapter on prayer. My basic ideas on prayer can be explained in this simple acrostic:

A doration
C onfession
T hanksgiving
S upplication

Adoration: How can we help but praise and worship God when we are recipients of the greatest love ever displayed on this earth or above it? We are invited into the presence of Almighty God through a gift of sacrificial love on His part.

Confession: Repentance and confession go hand in hand. Repentance means I am honestly sorry and ashamed for things I have done or said. Also involved in repentance is a "turning away from." It is not enough that I am sorry; I must strive not to commit that sin again. I will tell Jesus about my sin and ask for His help in ridding my life of it. This is confession.

Thanksgiving: "In everything give thanks . . ." (1

Thessalonians 5:18). This means for the good things and for the bad things—in *everything*.

Supplication: Recognizing that God is all powerful, we pray; aware of our failings but with the peaceful knowledge that God hears and will answer—this is supplication. We may ask God for something for ourselves, our family or loved ones, or people we do not personally know—heads of state or missionaries.

When all these elements are present in our prayers, we may be assured that we are praying Jesus' way.

Prayer: Talking With God

Our private communion with God is one of the highest privileges of the Christian life. I don't think true Christian maturity can be achieved without an effective prayer life.

A non-Christian, though deeply "religious," can speak frequent and eloquent prayers to his god, but there is no acceptance of them at the throne of grace, because they are not offered through the atoning blood of Jesus (*see* John 14:6). We Christians, on the other hand, are told in Hebrews 4:16, "Let us therefore draw near with confidence to the throne of grace, that we may receive mercy and may find grace to help in time of need." We have instant, unhindered access to our omnipotent God because we are trusting in Jesus.

"But you, when you pray, go into your inner room, and when you have shut your door, pray to your Father who is in secret, and your Father who sees in secret will repay you" (Matthew 6:6).

Romans 8:26–28 says:

And in the same way the Spirit also helps our weakness; for we do not know how to pray as we should, but the Spirit Himself intercedes for us with groanings too deep for words; and He who searches the hearts knows what the mind of the Spirit is, because

He intercedes for the saints according to the will of God. And we know that God causes all things to work together for good to those who love God, to those who are called according to His purpose.

Our cares and concerns need never be spoken of outside the privacy of our personal devotions. God hears and answers our prayers, because we are in His family.

I love having family devotions and prayer. I think husbands and wives should pray together. The Bible urges us to "bear one another's burdens . . ." (Galatians 6:2). Praying together binds our hearts in mutual concern for one another's needs, and that is a vital part of the close union which married couples are to share.

Prayer with other believers is also urged and we Christians need to unite our hearts in things of common interest and concern. It is a great comfort to me to know other brothers and sisters in Christ are praying for me and with me.

But, we must never forget that the prayer of a group is no more effective in the presence of God than your own personal prayers. Matthew 18:20 is often quoted when Christians gather for prayer: "For where two or three have gathered together in My name, there I am in their midst." When I was a new Christian, I was very puzzled about this verse. I recognized that Jesus, through His Holy Spirit, was present within me; therefore, how could two or three people more effectively bring about His presence than I did as I prayed alone? (*see* Colossians 1:27, " . . . Christ in you, the hope of glory").

I looked up Matthew 18 and to my relief, I found it has nothing at all to do with prayer. The passage deals with church discipline and the manner in which sinful members are to be rebuked. To use this verse in regard to prayer is to *make a pretext from a text you have lifted out of context!* It is not truth. If this verse had any reference to prayer, it would present some very difficult problems. It would hinder or eliminate our ability to pray privately.

There are also many wonderful verses and whole passages which may be used to support group prayer. I believe God's promise in 2 Chronicles 7:14 holds true today, as it did in the days of Solomon. James 5:13–16 tells us to pray for the sick. The beautiful passage of Hebrews 10:19–25 encourages us to join together in worship. Enjoying the fellowship of other believers is a rich blessing in the Christian life. Both individual and group prayer is essential to our Christian growth.

Keeping a Prayer Calendar

As you pray and study the Word, you may wish to keep a record of your prayer requests. A small spiral-ring notebook or stenographer's tablet works nicely. As you pray for a particular person or need, jot it down. Include the date of the request and make another column for the date of the answer to your prayer.

I have so many things and people to pray for that I find a weekly calendar meets my needs. I divide the requests between each of the seven days and in this way can pray regularly for a greater number of concerns. You may have one notebook and calendar for your private devotions and keep another for family worship.

Give Me a Few Good Men and Women

The Power of Prayer, by R. A. Torrey, is a dynamic book which I highly recommend for every Christian. It is a classic and is as relevant today as it was when it was written several decades ago. Doctor Torrey wrote:

Beyond a doubt, one of the great secrets of the unsatisfactoriness and superficiality and unreality and temporary character of many of our modern, so-called revivals is that so much dependence is put upon man's machinery and so little upon God's power, sought and obtained by

*the earnest, persistent, believing prayer that will not take
no for an answer.* We live in a day characterized by the
multiplication of man's machinery and the diminution of
God's power. The great cry of our day is work, work, work,
organize, organize, organize, give us some new society,
tell us some new methods, devise some new machinery;
*but the great need of our day is prayer, more prayer and
better prayer* . . . .

Great revivals always begin first in the hearts of a few
men and women whom God arouses by His Spirit to believe in Him as a living God, as a God who answers
prayer, and upon whose heart He lays a burden from
which no rest can be found except in importunate crying
unto God. Oh, may He, by His Spirit, lay such a burden
upon our hearts today. I believe He will.

And all I can add is, Amen.

6

Choosing to Go God's Way

When God created Adam and Eve, they were absolutely perfect. I am confident that he was gloriously handsome and she was far more gorgeous than any woman who has lived since. They were pure in spirit and, I venture to add, were not even bothered by weight problems—until, of course, that day when Eve was deceived and with Adam disobeyed, by eating of the forbidden fruit.

Through the centuries, their problems have become our problems. Perfection has become a multitude of imperfections; we all have our share! But, praise God, because of our cleansing through the shed blood of Jesus, we are now clothed in the righteousness of Christ. In God's sight, we are pure and holy. When we are so secure in our position in Christ, shouldn't our behavior reflect His glory?

Did Mother Really Make Her Do It?

I once had a woman tell me she couldn't help the way she was because her parents had spoiled her as a child and her behavior was all their fault.

All of us can look back through the years and put the blame for faults and shortcomings on our parents or some set of unfortunate circumstances. Modern psychology is trying to perpetuate this incomplete reasoning.

The Bible teaches something different: "When I was a child, I used to speak as a child, think as a child, reason as a child; when I became a man, I did away with childish things" (1 Corinthians 13:11). As adults, we are responsible for our actions. We have no excuse for continually perpetuating mistakes, whether made by our parents or by ourselves. When we are made aware of an area that needs changing, we must set about changing it. We can make the negative a positive influence in our lives.

Wishing Won't Make It Happen—Action Will!

Decisions to change—with God's help—are made by an act of our will. We decide to change; God helps us stick with it.

When I used to daydream as a child, I imagined all the wonderful things that would happen to me someday. Every night I looked for the first star to be seen from my window and, in childish fashion, made my wish. I tried hard to blow out every candle on my birthday cake, and tried to get the wishbone to break in my favor. But all the daydreams, stars, candles, and wishbones never changed a thing.

Some childish games and habits are hard to break when we become adults. Wishing didn't change my life, but Jesus did. He said, "Diane, follow Me, and allow Me to show you the mighty and wondrous things I have planned for you." But it was my decision of the will—my action—which allowed Him to show these wondrous things to me. He would never have forced Himself on me.

Who, Me?

Wondrous and *mighty* are not words that I would readily have used to describe my life some years back! I realize that, after having spoken to tens of thousands of women, having skated in the Ice Follies, and having done television programs, my life outwardly may appear to have a little more excitement and adventure than many others experience; but I have shared enough of myself in this book for you to see that inwardly wondrous and mighty are a bit removed from my experience! When I remember the poverty of my spiritual life before

I met Jesus, and compare it with the abundant riches I now have in Him, I can see my life becoming more wondrous and mighty as time passes.

Good, Better, or Best?

There really is no choice for the Christian about the direction his life is to take or the choice between right and wrong. If we are following Christ, we will always desire to do what is right. But many of us settle for what is good and often overlook what is best. Sometimes, it is said, the good becomes the enemy of the best. If we are going to give the best that is in us for any purpose, certainly God is worthy of the best.

But we must not confuse *the best* with *perfection*. We often either demand perfection from ourselves or alibi, "Well, nobody's perfect." That's right, but there is *the best* in everyone. It is not unrealistic to expect the best from ourselves if we are truthful. Isn't this the way it should be?

If the best should be the motivation of every Christian, why isn't it? Could it be that we think, "Well, God knows my weaknesses; He will forgive the fact that I only give Him the leftovers in my life"? Yes, God knows our weaknesses, and that is why He so graciously provided for them by giving us a power greater than our own.

But God sees beyond weakness—He sees our strength, our possibilities, our potential. Are we settling for less? Are we wasting unredeemable time on endeavors which will have no value in the Kingdom of God?

Many years ago, I memorized a little saying: "Only one life, 'twill soon be past; only what's done for Christ will last." What has lasting value and worth? Will the new automobile last for eternity? Or the house, or the washing machine? None of our material treasures will stand the test of time. Only treasures laid up in heaven will span the gap between the present and eternity.

Two problems which seem to keep us from realizing God's best are unbelief and disobedience.

Unbelief is a lack of trust in God and His Word, characterized by fear and lack of knowledge. Unbelief can paralyze God's power in our lives. The history of the Israelites provides a classic example of unbelief. Unbelief kept them in the wilderness for forty years when it was really a relatively short trip across the desert. Unbelief kept a whole generation from entering the Promised Land.

Unbelief paralyzes the believer when he thinks, "Yes, the promises of God are true—for others—but I doubt He can or will do the same for me."

When I was a fairly new Christian, I read many books and articles about what God had done in the lives of other Christians. Not all were famous persons. Some were unnoticed by the world around them—but not by God. After reading these stories I would think, "Oh, if only God could do that in *my* life." I was wishing for what I believed to be impossible for God to accomplish in *my* life. That's unbelief—thinking God's promises do not apply to me.

I could have experienced many of His blessings had I only believed Him for them. What caused my unbelief? Disobedience caused my unbelief. I robbed myself of much of the joy that was available to me in Christ. What I didn't experience because of lack of knowledge is one thing—but when I know what to do and refuse to act upon the knowledge I have, then I am being disobedient. All the promises and goodness of God are there—part of our inheritance—but often they go unclaimed because of our unbelief and disobedience.

Disobedience is not merely a collection of various acts or actions; it is a prevailing attitude. Many Christians live in a state of known disobedience or alienation from God for long periods of time. It is miserable to live in this state but, ironically, we choose it for ourselves.

God may at some time give us clear direction as to what He wants us to do; but we choose less for reasons of unbelief and disobedience. We may not consciously name unbelief as our reason; we may instead choose another direction because it appears more attractive, profitable, or secure. But the truth is, we don't believe God will follow through on His promises and provide for us to the end—and we miss the best.

Stress-Free Living

Walking by faith and not by feelings was a hard lesson for me to learn. Women are by nature more emotional beings than men. We tend to behave according to how we feel. Some days I feel better than other days. Feelings fluctuate according to hormones, metabolism, weather, checkbook balance, and a hundred other things. Therefore, feelings are not reliable.

Men tend toward being too self-sufficient, having been trained to think for themselves, make their own decisions, and seldom give in to emotions. Therefore, walking by faith is a difficult readjustment for them, too.

Our faith should be constant and consistent because God is the object of our faith; He does not waver or vary. Matthew 11:28–30 says:

Come to Me, all who are weary and heavy-laden, and I will give you rest. Take My yoke upon you, and learn from Me, for I am gentle and humble in heart; and you shall find rest for your souls. For My yoke is easy, and My load is light.

Going God's way need not be burdensome. It should bring rest to our souls and remove the tension and stress of living in this frantic society.

When I see nervous, uptight Christians in a state of panic about a multitude of things, my heart aches

for them. Jesus didn't live this way, and did not intend
for us to live in frenzy, either.

We worry so much—about anything and everything.
We even worry about whether we are "doing enough for
God"—trying desperately to live the Christian life—and
missing the joy of it completely.

Resting in the Lord does not mean sitting back and
doing nothing. Rather, it is being at peace, having our
assurance and confidence firmly entrenched in Jesus
Christ, our Savior and Lord.

The Amplified Bible paraphrases Matthew 11:28–30
this way:

Come to Me, all you who labor and are heavy-laden
and over burdened, and I will cause you to rest—I
will ease *and* relieve *and* refresh your souls. Take
My yoke upon you, and learn of Me; for I am gentle
(meek) *and* humble (lowly) in heart, and you will
find rest—relief, ease and refreshment and recreation and blessed quiet—for your souls. [Jeremiah
6:16.] For My yoke is wholesome (useful, good)—not
harsh, hard, sharp, or pressing, but comfortable, gracious and pleasant; and My burden is light *and* easy
to be borne.

These verses do not tell us that if we follow Him we
will be guaranteed a life of ease without problems or
difficulties. Scripture never teaches that.

Just before Jesus was betrayed, He counseled His disciples about what was going to take place shortly. His
words are still true for each of us: "I have told you these
things so that in Me you may have peace and confidence.
In the world you have tribulation and trials and distress
and frustration: but be of good cheer—take courage, be
confident, certain, undaunted—for I have overcome the
world. I have conquered it [for you]" (John 16:33
AMPLIFIED).

Choosing to go God's way enables each Christian to grow up in Christ; to conduct our lives in a manner that is worthy of our calling, and to experience the fullness and abundance of our all-sufficient Savior (*see* Ephesians 4).

Closet Cleaning

When the choice is made to follow Jesus and look to Him for guidance in every direction of life, we become aware of areas of our lives where change is indicated.

Of all my faults, perhaps the worst is that I am a "saver." I justify this by saying I am being both sentimental and practical. I keep some old clothes only because I like them—even though I know I'll never wear them again. I keep other things thinking the garments can be restyled or recycled. Of course I have to admit I seldom get around to it—so I pack and unpack many of the same clothes year after year.

Occasionally one of my children exclaims, "Oh, Mother, how could you ever have worn *that!*" I look at it, remembering how attractive it was when it was new. But now the design and style are dated.

Sometimes I laugh about it and toss the garment away. Other times, I clutch the dress to me and say, "I like it—it's still okay." Yet, in my heart, I know there is no use for it now. Old clothes can be like some of our habits and attitudes—out of style, useless, and just plain ugly!

God has been cleaning the closet of my mind for many years. He shows me what I need to change—selfish habits and negative attitudes that just aren't in style for my new life. Some have been easy to throw away; others I have wanted to cling to long after I knew they should not be a part of my life.

Why do we find security in hanging on to old clothes and old habits? What makes us resist change? When the Holy Spirit fills our life, how can we possibly fear change or what the future may hold? When He shows us some-

thing about ourselves that needs to be changed it is because He wants to replace it with something finer or
better. Change can actually be exciting when we are free
and open, allowing God to show us how great are all His
benefits. He gave us a new life and now new hopes,
goals, and motivation—regardless of our circumstances.

It is so human for us to look at our present or past
circumstances and give a list of excuses why particular
Christian principles do not apply to us. It is easy to look
at a healthy, wealthy saint of God and say, "No wonder
it's easy for him." However, we are rarely impaired in
our Christian growth by our physical limitations as we
are by our mental and emotional reservations.

Jessie, a dear friend and sister in Christ, has impaired
use of the right side of her body and difficulty in speaking. Life has not been easy for her, but she radiates the
love and sufficiency of Jesus Christ. She is a beautiful
example of faith to many whose physical circumstances
are far more pleasant than hers. We all have handicaps of
one kind or another, but they need not be hindrances.
We can touch the life of another person whatever—and
sometimes because of—our circumstances.

Cleaning the Closets of Our Minds

Some of the greatest deterrents to change often take
the form of fear, pride, and rigidity. For me, it is more a
problem of the latter. My confidence in God is strong
and I haven't had much of a problem with pride; however, for Mike the deterrent has primarily been pride.

Rigidity or a preestablished mind-set involves one's
frame of mind. In the area of resistance to change, it can
show itself by telling us, "But I've always done it this
way . . . . In my family, it's done . . . . When I was in
school . . . . In my church . . . ." and so on and on we
go, clinging to outmoded thought patterns.

Pride takes many forms. It can be rebellion against
God or another person. The change which is needed

may be obvious, but my pride won't let me admit that the problem is with me.

Fear can be a manifestation of pride, also. I fear God will not or cannot take care of me; result: pride—I can do it better myself. Let's face it; all are just plain old sins and we must deal with them accordingly.

When God says we are to have a sound mind, I believe He is saying that we are to have organized thinking, and use discernment and discretion in our dealings with the world.

Societal change is rampant and much of it is detrimental, obviously coming from unsound, ungodly minds. As Christians, we are warned in Scripture not to be impressed or swayed by slick, smooth-talking people whose doctrine, teaching, or life-style is inconsistent with God's Word.

Many have been wooed into cults because of the appeal of love, unity, and acceptance by the group. A human need was met, but the spiritual element was obviously not of God because of the mishandling of holy Scripture. I am not advocating change for the sake of change, but change for Jesus' sake.

Me Change First?

It is easy to think of all the things we would like to change in others. This is particularly true of husbands and wives. For years, I told myself, "If Mike would only change, I'd be so happy!" I had a mind-set and kept my attention focused on his faults.

God showed me that in our family I needed to be the first one to change. I had the responsibility to be the person He had commanded me to be. If change were to come in Mike's life, it would be the result of the Holy Spirit working within him and not Diane working from the outside.

Initially, I resisted the changes that I knew were necessary. It seems to go against our grain to think that there is something wrong with us. It's far easier to see faults in others.

> And why do you look at the speck in your brother's eye, but do not notice the log that is in your own eye? Or how can you say to your brother, "Let me take the speck out of your eye," and behold, the log is in your own eye? You hypocrite, first take the log out of your own eye, and then you will see clearly enough to take the speck out of your brother's eye.
>
> Matthew 7:3–5

This is an often-quoted, seldom-applied passage! I don't mind admitting to a few specks in my eye, but a log!

I once had an eye injury where a tiny speck of the cornea sloughed off. Both eyes had to be bandaged because the slightest movement of the good eye caused movement with intense pain in the injured eye. I could not function in any capacity effectively until that minute speck had healed.

Each time God makes me aware of another distasteful "speck" in my personality, I cannot function at 100 percent capacity until the proper measures for healing (confession) and growth (repentance and change) have taken place.

Negative attitudes are disastrous—mentally, emotionally, physically, and spiritually. Pride, jealousy, envy, gossip, lying, dishonesty, and self-pity all reap havoc in the life of any person who allows those feelings and actions to dominate him. These characteristics are not of God; they are a snare of the enemy.

Many circumstances in our lives may be beyond our control, but how we deal with them is largely our choice. God gives us much freedom of choice. How wisely we exercise our choices will determine how well we succeed in solving the problems which confront us.

I often recommend a little pamphlet called *Your Reactions Are Showing* by Dr. J. Allen Petersen. He explains how we can plan our actions at any given time but, by our reactions, we show what we are really like. How do you think you would react consciously and unconsciously to these situations?

Your mate's faults
Criticism, both constructive and destructive
Past circumstances
Hurts or injustice
Unacceptable behavior in your children
Death of a friend or loved one

Would your reactions now be different from those of a year ago—five years ago—before you became a Christian? We can resist change, strike out against our problems, or use them as opportunities to trust God more completely.

Dealing With Unexpected Change

We have considered situations where we may have reacted negatively or positively to particular attitudes or situations. We exercise a degree of choice when God confronts us with a particular personality trait. However, there are many changes which occur during the course of a lifetime over which we may have little or no control— the loss of a mate or loved one, divorce or marital conflict, loss of employment, an accident or illness.

There are times when our whole world seems to come crashing down around us. We are gripped by fear for the future, and sometimes are hostile to a God who would allow such a thing to befall us.

In times of stress or uncertainty, we must claim God's promises for care and provision. Many benefits go unclaimed because we do not seek God for them or abide in His love. Instead, we battle Him in stubborn, self-willed defiance. As long as we exercise our will in refusing to accept our circumstance, we will forfeit God's peace and comfort. There will be no resiliency or hope; the blessing of God will be missed. We have chosen to reject the provisions of God which, in reality, are the very things we so desperately search for.

Changes are hard to face. But, if we face them with fear and dread, the results will be despair and despondency. Conversely, if we apply what is available to us in Christ, we have the assurance that "perfect love casts out all fear" (*see* 1 John 4:18).

Other Scriptures which will assure us of the fact are Philippians 4:4–9; Hebrews 13:20, 21; James 1:2–5; Deuteronomy 29:29; Jeremiah 29:11–14, 33:3 (God's "phone number").

A variety of circumstances contribute to our spiritual growth. We will be happier if we count the past as a blessing from which we have learned a great deal. Change can be fun when our motive is to live fully and victoriously for the One who makes harmonious changes a blessing to be enjoyed.

7

Open to His Leading

As we seek to know God in intimate daily fellowship, we begin to learn more about ourselves. Slowly He begins to reveal to us what we are really like in our old sin nature. We are given a new nature at the time of regeneration (new birth), but that old sin nature is still present and has to be dealt with on occasion. These self-discoveries can be joyful, but most of them are painful. Truth can be both.

If a list were kept of our self-discoveries, I imagine we would need two columns—one for credits, the other for debits. God brings these truths about ourselves to our attention for a purpose—to give us the ability to grow and mature in the faith and practice for daily living.

The Christian life simply cannot be lived apart from Christ. After all, He is the only One who ever lived it perfectly! In 2 Corinthians 12:9, 10, Paul relates what Jesus told him in a time of Paul's distress:

And He has said to me, "My grace is sufficient for you, for power is perfected in weakness." Most gladly, therefore, I will rather boast about my weaknesses, that the power of Christ may dwell in me. Therefore I am well content with weaknesses, with insults, with distresses, with persecutions, with difficulties, for Christ's sake; for when I am weak, then I am strong.

Past mistakes cannot be changed, but they can be of great benefit to us if we view them as opportunities which Jesus can use to teach us a valuable lesson. I imagine I have learned far more from my mistakes than I have from my successes. I once had a student attend one of my seminars who shared her motto about the past: "I view the past as I would the rearview mirror in the car. Look in it often enough to go forward, but not so much that you run into the ditch!"

I like that motto. It is the best way I know to view past mistakes. We can learn from our mistakes; they can contribute to our growth in God's grace. But most of our time should be spent looking forward.

Guilty Verdict, Sentence Commuted

When Christ gave Himself to be the sacrifice for our sins, the act was final—redemption was complete. Jesus said, "It is finished!" (John 19:30). What remains is for the believer to appropriate the finished work of Christ, by agreeing with God concerning the sin in his life. Remember 1 John 1:9? "If we confess our sins, he is faithful and just to forgive us our sins, and to cleanse us from all unrighteousness" (KJV).

As mistakes and areas of sinfulness are brought to our attention, we must confess them immediately. We need to right any wrong done to another person, and to thank God that He is changing the direction of our lives. But then we must—and this is of equal importance—forget it. It is over, God has forgiven us, and we must not keep punishing ourselves for past errors.

Psalms 103:12 says, "As far as the east is from the west, so far hath he removed our transgressions from us" (KJV). If God has forgiven us, how can we do otherwise than to forgive ourselves?

Dealing in Specifics

A daily confession with the quick statement, "Lord, forgive my sins today," is not enough. It does not recognize the problem areas which hinder the work of the Holy Spirit in our lives. We can easily fall into the trap of praying in generalities, instead of identifying specific attitudes or actions. God deals in specifics.

As I examined my personal attitudes, I found many

carnal areas. I used to try to justify my actions or attitudes by blaming them on unfair treatment by someone else. I was wrong. My actions and my attitudes are my responsibility. If I act unkindly in response to an unkind act, that's my problem. I cannot justify blaming someone else.

The full realization of what we are in our old sin nature, apart from the grace of God, is an overwhelming thing. But, praise God, we can lay our petitions and problems at the foot of the cross and claim the shed blood of our Redeemer to cover our sins!

Little Sinners Versus Big Sinners

There is sometimes confusion in dealing with sin actions and attitudes. We tend to categorize sins—all the way from little white lies to the most hideous crimes. If we have never committed a really serious crime, we don't consider ourselves much of a sinner—even though we stretch the truth regularly, speed on the highway, and cheat a bit on our income tax.

Certainly, we rationalize, overt acts of wrongdoing deserve stronger punishment than attitudes formed in one's mind. It is a very human trait to think, *Wow, I'm sure glad I'm not like that person.*

And with a very self-righteous and critical spirit, we begin to tear mentally that person to shreds! In truth, our attitude is as sinful before God as that person's actions. We are both sinners in the sight of God and need His forgiveness and cleansing. My attitudes have been a real stumbling block to me. I love God, have a tremendous desire to study the Word, but have had times of real discouragement and frustration in my Christian walk. When I was a new Christian, I questioned God about why He didn't change my whole marriage situation instantaneously. He is all powerful; it would not have been beyond His capability. Truthfully, many times I grumbled and complained before the Lord, telling Him

He was wasting a lot of valuable time by not doing what I thought He should!

Oh, the way we abuse the privilege of prayer! After giving God all my opinions, I would sigh and say, "Well, may Thy will be done." Herein lies the crux of the matter. I venture to say many Christians do not know what it means to pray, "Thy will be done," or to *live* life according to God's will. It is a pivotal point in our Christian experience which will determine the extent of our success in other areas of our lives.

Praying for God's will to be done means praying that His ultimate purposes will be accomplished. We sometimes tack that on the end of our prayers, thinking that if He doesn't answer them the way we hope He will, we have backed up our disappointment by quoting Scripture!

Praying this way is really praying with an unbelieving heart. Praying that God's will be done really means having the confident assurance that He is in control of every situation.

What Is God's Will for You?

Many women have told me they are unhappy being "just housewives" because they feel they cannot know God's will for their lives! Somewhere, somehow, we have received and passed on the misconception that only evangelists, missionaries, preachers, scholars, and "professional Christians" are in God's will. They have cornered the market and there is no room left for the rest of us!

God's will extends to *every one* of His children. He does not play favorites or measure success on the same scale the secular world does. I am confident that there are "professionals" who are as far outside of God's will as those Christians who only warm the bench on Sunday morning. But, I'm glad to say, that is not for me to judge.

I have enough to do handling the responsibilities God has given me!

I have outlined God's attributes, including His sovereignty. I have confidence in God because I know the Scriptures teach He is sovereign. The Scriptures also teach that I am required to live my life in a responsible way, one that will bring glory and honor to Him. This statement at first glance may seem to be contradictory, yet in fact it is true. In some way in the mystery of God (*see* Deuteronomy 29:29), He created us with the freedom to make choices. If we lean toward sovereignty alone, we can slip into a passive, uninvolved Christian existence that in essence says, "*Que sera, sera*— whatever will be, will be," and there is nothing for me to do. I have even heard it said, "If God wants me to witness to someone, He can send them to my door!" I don't see this attitude as one coming from the Word of God or the illumination of the mind by the Holy Spirit. We would be imbalanced in our attitude toward our own personal responsibility to honor God through our actions. God's will is not prevailing in this kind of life.

In order to know God's will in your life, I believe the need is for every professing Christian to conduct his life according to the directives given us in the Bible. Four words stand out in my mind as the necessary elements for living in the center of God's will for our lives: *seek, love, keep,* and *abide.*

"But seek first His Kingdom and His righteousness; and all these things shall be added to you" (Matthew 6:33).

"We love, because He first loved us" (1 John 4:19).

"If you love Me, you will keep My commandments" (John 14:15).

"Abide in Me, and I in you. As the branch cannot bear fruit of itself, unless it abides in the vine, so neither can you, unless you abide in Me" (John 15:4).

Seeking God's Kingdom begins at the time of conversion and continues throughout our Christian lives. We find Him when we are born again, but throughout the years we seek to know Him more and more intimately. He must have first place in our lives. To give Him anything less is to dishonor Him and devalue the person and work of Jesus Christ.

"We love, because He first loved us." God's capacity to love knows no bounds. His love is pure, unselfish, a supernatural gift to us, revealed in the supreme act of love—Christ's death and Resurrection. He loves us in spite of what we are, not because we measure up to His standards.

Human love is often selfish and possessive, dependent on emotions and returned only when we feel loved. In Jesus, we receive a new capacity to love. We can love even the unlovable, because Christ is now loving others through us.

"If you love Me, you will keep My commandments." Do we really love Him? Are we fully aware of what He has done for us? Is there within our hearts a desire to please Him? Do we yearn for spiritual growth and maturity? Then we will keep His commandments. We will show our love by the quality of our lives. Christ in us can be joy never ceasing, a radiance that shines forth and brings peace to our hearts.

The closer I stay to Jesus, the more I realize He is all I need. He has never failed me, hurt me, or forsaken me and He never will. As I abide in Him, He has the complete freedom to reproduce His life through me. I will bear fruit.

I have heard it said that the fruit of a Christian is another Christian—leading a person to Christ. It is my understanding from Scripture that the fruit of a Christian is the Christian life. The word *Christian* means "Christ in one."

When Christ lives in the believer through the indwelling presence of the Holy Spirit, and the believer yields the control of His life to Christ, the result of that abiding life is "the fruit of the Spirit"—love, joy, peace, patience, kindness, goodness, faithfulness, gentleness, and self-control (*see* Galatians 5:22, 23). The fruitful Christian life cannot be lived apart from Christ.

There have been times during the past few years when I was not abiding in Jesus; when I was not studying my Bible or having an effective prayer life. Those were miserable periods when self-pity and anxiety almost overwhelmed me. I have learned from experience that I cannot live apart from Jesus. Without Him, as John 15:5 says, I can do nothing. I am incomplete and, oh, so very alone.

We have glimpsed some of the many gifts God has for us. In my own life, what I needed most were new thoughts and attitudes. First came the willingness to open my life to Christ's control and then the learning process of trusting in His leading. My new attitudes and thought life came about as a direct result of abiding in Christ. This is so crucial to the success of our Christian life that I want to develop it in more detail.

Jesus said to His disciples—and to you and me:

I AM the true vine, and My Father is the vine-dresser. Every branch in Me that does not bear fruit, He takes away; and every branch that bears fruit, He prunes it, that it may bear more fruit. You are already clean because of the word which I have spoken to you. Abide in Me, and I in you. As the branch cannot bear fruit of itself, unless it abides in the vine, so neither can you, unless you abide in Me. I am the vine, you are the branches; he who abides in Me, and I in him, he bears much fruit; for apart from Me you can do nothing. If anyone does not abide in Me, he is thrown away as a branch, and dries up; and they gather them, and cast them into the fire, and they are burned. If you abide in Me, and My words abide in you, ask whatever you wish, and it shall be

done for you. By this is My Father glorified, that you
bear much fruit, and so prove to be My disciples.

John 15:1–8

During staff training with Campus Crusade for Christ
in the summer of 1974, our morning devotions on this
passage of Scripture were given by the Reverend Ronald
C. Dunn, at that time pastor of the McArthur Boulevard
Baptist Church in Irving, Texas. Our tapes on these mes-
sages have continued to minister to both Mike and me.
In the following paragraphs, I'd like to share some of the
Reverend Dunn's insights, as well as my own.

In essence, Scripture relates that Jesus gives three in-
vitations to mankind. The first invitation is, "Come unto
Me" for pardon, peace, rest—for salvation. The second
is, "Follow Me." After we come to Jesus, we are to follow Him in service and discipleship. Third, Jesus says,
"Abide in Me." When we consider these three invita-
tions, we have the scope of the Christian life. "Come to
Me; follow Me; abide in Me." Each grows out of the
other; each indicates a deeper, more intimate relationship with our Lord Jesus.

In a certain sense, every believer is already abiding in
Jesus, just as there is a sense in which every person who
has found the Lord is still seeking Him. But here Jesus is
speaking to people who are already *in* Him, telling them
to "abide in Me."

Notice that He doesn't tell them (and us) to "abide
with Me." There is quite a difference between the words
with and *in*. We are not coming to Him for periodic companionship or aid in time of distress. We are to abide in
Him always. Abiding *in* Him is to be a lifelong process.

Colossians 2:6, 7 reads, "As you therefore have received Christ Jesus the Lord, so walk *in* Him, having
been firmly rooted and now being built up *in* Him and
established *in* your faith, just as you were instructed, and
overflowing with gratitude" (author's italics).

Service-Station Christianity

Jesus is telling us that He wants us to be totally immersed in Him. He wants to be our total environment; we are to find in Him everything we need to live. He is our world and the very air that we breathe.

It is sad how often we do not heed this call to abide. We rush to Him when there is an urgent need for help, strength, comfort, or guidance, as if He were the local service station—a place where we swing by for a fill-up or a dollar's worth, depending on the magnitude of the task we are facing. Then we don't come to Him again until we are registering "empty."

Many times when Scripture refers to Christ's power within us, the Greek word *"dunamis"* is used. This is sometimes translated "dynamite." Ron Dunn says, "We sure see a lot of dynamite Christians around. You know the kind—they make a lot of noise, stir up a lot of dust, and it's over in just a minute!"

But he went on to explain another word which comes from the root word *dunamis*. It is "dynamo"—a continual source of energy. And that's what Jesus is. He is not a stick of dynamite which gives us a charge once in a while; He is a dynamo—a continual source of energy.

In John 15, He is saying, "Live in Me the life of a branch—draw all your strength and vitality, all of your being from Me."

Is Rest Laziness?

As I work in my garden, and watch the new buds and bulbs come to life, I wonder about all the activity going on underneath the surface. The strength and sustaining life of these plants comes from beneath the surface, where they are nourished in private, hidden from sight. Their growth and productivity depend on what we cannot see—union with the vine, the root.

When we abide in Christ, the responsibility for success, results, and production is on Him. This doesn't mean that we are to be passive or to just sit around. The Apostle Paul is a beautiful example of the abiding life—and who has been busier than Paul?

Abiding gives us "rest," but idleness or inactivity is not mentioned. The word *rest* literally means "the releasing of a tight bowstring"—the releasing of tension. We can work until we are exhausted physically and still be at rest. Why? Because there is no tautness, no stress. If we wish to see fruitfulness produced in our lives, we need to learn how to abide—how to live the life of a branch.

There seem to be three essential qualifications for, or characteristics involved in, abiding in Jesus. These three elements are reflected in the relationship between God the Father and Jesus while He was on earth—confession, communication, and commitment.

We must confess our inadequacies. Jesus said that apart from Him we can do nothing. Speaking of His union with the Father, He said, "I can of Myself do nothing" (*see* John 8:28).

You may be thinking, "Oh, I have done many things." I am not saying—and Jesus didn't say—that apart from Him you would not have activity. He said you wouldn't have fruit. Work—activity—is something man produces; only God produces fruit.

In the Book of Galatians, Paul speaks of work as being a product of the flesh, and of fruit as being a product of the Spirit. There can be a lot of work and activity with no fruit. What we produce can seem to be something great in our eyes and in the eyes of the world. But Jesus says unless He is producing through our human availability, we can do nothing of lasting value in the Kingdom of God.

Paul makes a contrast between the Christian who works in the power of the flesh and one who works in the power of the Spirit:

According to the grace of God which was given to me, as a wise master builder I laid a foundation, and another is building upon it. But let each man be careful how he builds upon it. For no man can lay a foundation other than the one which is laid, which is Jesus Christ. Now if any man builds upon the foundation with gold, silver, precious stones, wood, hay, straw, each man's work will become evident; for the day will show it, because it is to be revealed with fire; and the fire itself will test the quality of each man's work. If any man's work which he has built upon it remains, he shall receive a reward. (1 Corinthians 3:10–14)

Paul is telling us that when a person is saved, God lays a foundation and that foundation is Jesus Christ. A foundation is not the entire building, yet some Christians act as though the foundation is all that is necessary. That's not what the Bible teaches. Scripture teaches that we are to erect a superstructure of Christian living, being careful to use the kinds of materials that have everlasting quality.

The world today often emphasizes quantity over quality. God doesn't measure our fruitfulness by the quantity of our labor but by the quality of our life. We simply *can't* impress the Creator of the universe with the size of our production. He is interested in what sort of materials we use. If we are not abiding in Jesus, our efforts to build consist of wood, hay, and straw.

Communication is the second element involved in living the life of a branch. A branch must stay in constant contact with the vine; if not, it withers away. Can you imagine a branch so busy making fruit that it has no time for the vine? We, like the vine, must keep the lines of communication open, through prayer and study of the Word.

Robert Murray McCheyne once said, "What a man is in

his prayer closet is what he is." We are never closer to Jesus in public than we are in private. We must have our quiet time in order to be a fruit-producing branch of the Vine.

If our gift to God is the life we live, it must be one of commitment, availability, and oneness with Jesus. Our responsibility as a branch is to place ourselves at the disposal of the Vine. He is our reason for being.

I am firmly convinced that when we are abiding in Jesus, there will be fruit. It is simply the outward expression of the inward nature of our lives—the natural outgrowth of a life lived *in* Him.

Just as the vine does not have to struggle to bear its fruit, God does not intend for us to worry about whether or not we are doing enough for Him. We will work hard, but the fruit will be borne naturally and spontaneously.

God measures our faith by our availability and attitude. If we abide in Him, we can come to the end of each day filled with peace, praying, "Lord, I am Yours; I am available. I'm just a branch, abiding in the Vine."

8
Divinely Designed

Fashion commentators sometimes use such phrases as, "This gown has divine lines," or "This heavenly creation was designed by . . . ." And six months later, it is out of style!

God is our divine Designer. We are His heavenly creations—and what He designs never goes out of style! We are unique, priceless, one-of-a-kind originals.

We human beings have great value and worth, with a potential that is largely untapped. It's time we as Christians step forth in style and individuality, making an impact on society for Jesus Christ.

Sometimes I am struck by the fact that many Christians don't appear as happy as non-Christians. An overwhelming number look sorrowful, afraid, ill at ease, or just plain dowdy. I find myself thinking, *But, Lord, it shouldn't be this way.* Who could be more radiant than a child of the King? Since we are clothed in the righteousness of Jesus, shouldn't the result be an inner beauty which never fades, a kind of aura which reflects the serenity of our Lord?

I am happy, though, that there are many instances when I meet a person whose glow is unmistakably the Spirit of Christ. There is sometimes an almost indelible mark upon the countenance which identifies that person as a true believer.

What are the imperishable qualities which contribute to inner beauty? I believe the basic elements of inner beauty are the same as for outward beauty—genetics, nutrition, and careful grooming. The Christian has all three present and available when he or she is born into the family of God.

Genetically, we are perfect. We were born into God's family through incorruptible, imperishable seed (*see*

1 Peter 1:23), and we will never die. We possess a royal heritage. Made holy through Christ's blood, our bodies are the temple of the Holy Spirit. We are 100 percent pure and clean in the eyes of God. No one but a Christian can make such a statement.

Nutritionally, we have every element available to keep our spiritual bodies healthy and strong. Jesus said in John 6:35, "I am the bread of life; he who comes to Me shall not hunger, and he who believes in Me shall never thirst." "And all ate the same spiritual food; and all drank the same spiritual drink, for they were drinking from a spiritual rock which followed them; and the rock was Christ" (1 Corinthians 10:3, 4).

Psalms 119:103 says, "How sweet are Thy words to my taste! Yes, sweeter than honey to my mouth!" Related verses are Isaiah 55:2; Revelation 2:7; and Deuteronomy 8:3.

In 1 Peter 2:2, we are told to desire the pure milk of the Word. Other verses in Scripture refer to new Christians as babes who need milk, as in Hebrews 5:12–14:

> For though by this time you ought to be teachers, you have need again for some one to teach you the elementary principles of the oracles of God, and you have come to need milk and not solid food. For every one who partakes only of milk is not accustomed to the word of righteousness, for he is a babe. But solid food is for the mature, who because of practice have their senses trained to discern good and evil. (*See also* 1 Corinthians 3:2.)

"Thy words were found and I ate them, And Thy words became for me a joy and the delight of my heart; For I have been called by Thy name, O Lord God of hosts" (Jeremiah 15:16). God's Word is the only spiritual food we need in order to live.

Careful Grooming is essential to the way we present

Christ. Whenever we see persons who are poised, well mannered, and attractively attired, we know they do not look that way by accident. Their appearance is the result of time spent in careful grooming.

When we meet godly men or women whose lives reflect Christlike characteristics, we know it is because they know and reverence Jesus Christ, not only as Savior but also as Lord. They abide in Him daily, walk in Him, trust in Him. They are holy because He is holy. They are kind because He is kindness. They are showing forth the results of a life lived in Jesus. The person whose life is dedicated to serving Christ will increasingly reflect the characteristics of the One to whom he wishes to bring honor and glory.

Inside Looking Out

Inner beauty develops within each individual according to that person's willingness to be used as God chooses. As a person matures in faith and practice, he becomes more beautiful inwardly.

One of the most beautiful Christians I have ever met is a man in his nineties, Seiichi Ozeki from Nagoya, Japan. We could not speak the same language, but we all belong to the same Lord. Mr. Ozeki's countenance shines with the love of Jesus. He has been an ordained elder for more than seventy-five years. He ministers to others and has been very successful in business. He abides in Jesus and the result is that Jesus has been a dynamo in his life—a continual source of energy, a continuous life-giving force.

The Fruit of the Spirit

Inner beauty develops as admirable qualities become a natural part of our personality. There are scores of exemplary traits found in Scripture. I have listed a number of positive attributes with their negative coun-

terparts and Scripture references in Appendix A in the
back of the book.

In the following pages I am going to amplify only
the nine characteristics found in Galatians 5:22, 23,
known as the fruit of the Spirit. As you read these characteristics and the ones listed in the appendix, prayerfully
consider what the Scriptures say concerning each one. It
would also be helpful to make notes as to how you may
wish to implement these qualities in your life.

Inner beauty is reflected in our thoughts, habit patterns, conduct at home, office, church, and social gather-
ings. Wherever we are, whatever we are doing, as Christians we cannot separate our life from the life of Christ.

The virtues listed in the Galatians passage are produced through the work of the Holy Spirit. For clarity, I
have divided the nine traits into three categories:

1. Love, joy, peace
2. Patience, kindness, goodness
3. Faithfulness, gentleness, self-control

Love, Joy, Peace

Love, joy, and peace are the inner mental assurances
of Jesus' presence within our souls. It is the deep union
of our spirits which goes beyond outward circumstances.
When we truly love God and others, we fulfill John
15:12; "This is My commandment, that you love one
another, just as I have loved you." We have joy in the fact
we are loved and accepted by God and privileged to
serve Him.

The word *love* is often misused and perverted today. It
is common to think of love as only feelings of physical
attraction, as gratification of the senses. "I love the taste
of . . . the smell of . . . the sight of . . . ." This kind of
passion is not present in biblical terms. We are developing here our capacity to appreciate and respond in earnest thankfulness to God for His mercy and love to us.

If a person is not loving within his heart, he will never

reach emotional maturity. The selfish, self-centered person is immature and cannot understand or refuses to meet the needs of another person. His self-love blocks out the ability to truly love others and to honestly and fully love God.

Like God, love cannot be seen, but we know of its existence by its effect. No better description of love has ever been written than the one in 1 Corinthians 13:4–7 in the Living Bible:

> Love is very patient and kind, never jealous or envious, never boastful or proud, never haughty or selfish or rude. Love does not demand its own way. It is not irritable or touchy. It does not hold grudges and will hardly even notice when others do it wrong. It is never glad about injustice, but rejoices whenever truth wins out. If you love someone you will be loyal to him no matter what the cost. You will always believe in him, always expect the best of him, and always stand your ground in defending him.

The qualities mentioned in this passage of Scripture are the qualities of a mature Christian person. These characteristics are not present in a selfish, immature individual. A selfish attitude is displeasing to God and is a sin. In order to be overcome, it must be faced as a sin and confessed.

Maturity is relative. A man may be a successful businessman and an overgrown baby as a husband. A woman may be effective in jobs or organizations outside the home and still be a selfish, childish, miserable wife. No matter what kind of success we may have elsewhere, if we do not have a loving spirit, we have missed one of life's greatest happinesses.

Joy within the soul grows out of the love relationship we have with Jesus. Peace follows, and for me, it is the quiet confidence that nothing in life can separate me from the love of Jesus. With these three manifestations of Christ in my life I can live daily in genuine harmony with my Lord and others.

Patience, Kindness, Goodness

Patience, kindness, and goodness are the outward evidence of our inward union with Christ. Patience is sometimes also translated "long-suffering."

We live in an impatient world. Years ago, if a person missed the stagecoach, he'd just get the one next month. But now when someone misses his slot in the revolving door, he can barely cope with it! Our technological advances have created a high-pressured society where a patient, long-suffering person is hard to find.

Romans 5:3 says that tribulation brings about patience. That comforts me because I have experienced tribulation, trials, and testing. Patience is not a product of my old nature. Patience is Jesus in me. When I am patient, kind, or good, I thank God for the perfecting influence He has in my actions.

Kindness seems to be missing in many lives. Rudeness and irritability often occur. I want a kindly disposition, not a disposition based on reactions to cranky individuals. I want kindness, drawn from a heart of love which recognizes that others have weaknesses and difficulties of which I am unaware. Kindness is seen in actions, a pleasing disposition, a mild temper, and a calm spirit. It would be difficult to possess true kindness apart from Jesus.

God is goodness (*see* Matthew 19:17). Our ability to be, do, and act good is impossible apart from Him. Goodness shows itself in moral excellence and true compassion for others. Purity in motive, virtue, and integrity are all implied as the evidence of goodness in a person's life.

A nonbeliever can do acts of charity for others, but in the eyes of God, only His children possess goodness. In

Acts 11:24, Barnabas was called a "good man" because he was filled with the Holy Ghost.

Faithfulness, Gentleness, Self-Control

These three traits represent Christian conduct. Faithfulness, as it is used in this verse, refers not to our faith in God but in our trustworthiness toward others. We Christians are to keep our word as our bond. We are to keep another person's confidences. We are to have fidelity in marriage, in business, in friendships, and in family relationships.

There is no pretense about us, no phoniness. We are honest, loyal, law-abiding citizens. If anyone should be the example of righteous living, certainly it is the Christian.

Gentleness is often mistaken as only a feminine trait, but it is one quality I most admire in a man—a real gentleman, tenderhearted, courteous, and honorable. *Meek* is sometimes used interchangeably with gentleness.

Meekness in today's usage is frequently confused with weakness. Biblically speaking, to be meek was a strength in one's character, as is humility. It is not a weakness to esteem others before yourself, yet some segments of society are training already self-centered persons to be more assertive and demanding of their rights.

Can you picture a family at the dinner table fighting over who gets the biggest piece of meat, each thinking he deserves it most? Mankind is greedy and harsh enough by nature without added training in how to dominate and manipulate others.

If we are gentle in our behavior toward others, we show respect for them. It doesn't matter which economic class they are in; we won't personally esteem some more highly than others. In matters of etiquette, we should familiarize ourselves with some of the finer social graces. A gentle person will have the self-confidence to handle himself properly in all situations.

We need to practice politeness and courtesy at home. I firmly believe that as representatives of Jesus, our conduct should always demonstrate the finest elements of poise and grace, both publicly and privately.

Self-control means accepting responsibility for our actions, being sure they are in line with God's rules for Christian behavior. A good analogy on self-control is shown in Ephesians 5:18: "And do not get drunk with wine, for that is dissipation, but be filled with the Spirit." Alcohol controls behavior, but a Christian's behavior is to be controlled by the Holy Spirit.

Intemperance in any area of life can bring about a controlling influence. We are to have all of our passions, desires, and appetites under control. Indulgences, excesses, or extremes in anything can be harmful to our Christian influence.

Moderation and balance keep us in the proper frame of mind to be in control of ourselves. This doesn't take the fun out of being a Christian—it adds to it. It gives us freedom to grow and develop in the finest sense of the word. True freedom and liberation are found within boundaries which God in His protective mercy has given us. With control, we can keep a check on emotional outbursts and even petty annoyances.

History paints a dim picture of persons and nations who have lost self-control; destruction has usually been the result. Remember Rome—where "anything goes" and eventually everything went? We are seeing the same pattern in our country today.

The atmosphere of every home, school, business, and recreational area would be more enjoyable and productive if everyone practiced honest self-control. I am thankful God enables us to be in control of ourselves.

Friendliness, Humor

I'd like to add two personality traits to the biblical list—friendliness and humor. I am basically quite shy and reserved. Unfortunately, this is occasionally interpreted as aloofness or unfriendliness when just the opposite is true. Shyness is a part of some persons' temperaments, but God can give boldness where it is needed. I still have difficulty in this area sometimes, but I know the doubts about my ability are from Satan and not from my Lord.

Some days in our Christian life we will know success; other days, we are likely to fall flat on our faces. God has given us the freedom to fail, and failure is as much a part of maturation as is success.

A sense of humor helps maintain one's perspective about life—especially during trying times. I love the proverb "A joyful [merry] heart is good medicine . . ." (Proverbs 17:22).

Happy memories often involve laughter. God gave us life to be enjoyed, not merely endured. There is so much in life to enjoy if we will just open ourselves to the good things around us.

"But thanks be to God, who always leads us in His triumph in Christ, and manifests through us the sweet aroma of the knowledge of Him in every place. For we are a fragrance of Christ to God among those who are being saved and among those who are perishing" (2 Corinthians 2:14, 15). A merry heart produces a friendly smile, which in turn, makes a day lovely.

Truly we are blessed—new life, new hope, new ability to live in harmony with God and all mankind. May the beauty of our Lord fill your life and may you be an inspiration to a searching world.

9

Beauty Is More Than Skin Deep

We Americans live in a star-studded society. Beauty is big business—and by the time we reach our preteens, we know whether we have it or not! If we do, we are "in"; if we don't, we have been made painfully aware of the fact by our peers.

Perhaps at some time you have cried or pretended peer teasing didn't matter. But the truth is it does matter and emotional scars can develop which will last a lifetime.

In the previous chapter I outlined what I believe are the three basic elements for both inner and outward beauty: genetics, nutrition, and careful grooming, which will be covered in the next chapter.

Like true inner beauty, the beauty which is reflected on the surface is the result of several things all working together to give a person physical attractiveness. It is interesting to bear in mind, as you read this chapter, that without first developing the Christlike qualities previously discussed, no amount of good looks will carry you happily through life. Egotism and selfishness will destroy the beauty one possesses in the eyes of other people.

Recently, I met a friend I had not seen in many years. As we were visiting she told me she had had plastic surgery on her rather prominent nose. She said she had been very self-conscious about it all her life—but I had never noticed that her nose was large. In my mind, she is one of the loveliest, most gracious ladies I have ever known. Beauty really is in the eye of the beholder!

I have another friend who has all the physical attributes one could ever wish for, but her conversation is constantly punctuated with vulgar words. This habit destroys her beauty in the eyes of everyone she meets.

As Christians, we are ambassadors of the King of Kings and the Lord of Lords. We are royalty. We should not only act like it but we should also reflect our relationship to Christ in the way we care for ourselves. I believe we Christians should be the healthiest, best-looking people in the world!

Genetics

We have no control over our basic physical features. Our looks are just one of those many things we must accept. We can, however, make the most of what we have.

I am eternally grateful that God looks upon our hearts and loves and accepts us as we are. But if our hearts' desire is to give God our very best, shouldn't that also be carried over in the way we care for our bodies? "Do you not know that you are a temple of God, and that the Spirit of God dwells in you?" (1 Corinthians 3:16). "I urge you therefore, brethren, by the mercies of God, to present your bodies a living and holy sacrifice, acceptable to God, which is your spiritual service of worship" (Romans 12:1). (*See also* 1 Corinthians 6:19; 2 Corinthians 6:16.)

Some Christians do not think their outward appearance matters—only what is on the inside counts. If we think this way, are we really taking time to consider how close the ties are between a healthy body and a healthy mind? How we care for our bodies is often a reflection of the image we have of ourselves. It seems to me that disregarding the needs of the body is dishonoring or devaluing God who resides there.

We all know that "an ounce of prevention is worth a pound of cure." We tune our cars' engines, paint our houses, polish our silver, brass, and copper. Lawns are mowed, gardens watered, leaves raked. Shouldn't we deserve equal—better—care than all of our *things?*

Maybe we can't do anything about our genetics, but we can do plenty about the other two items on the list—nutrition and grooming.

Introduction to Nutrition

In a recent survey taken by the Louis Harris Organization, it was shown that the majority of people questioned knew what they should do in order to stay healthy. About 40 percent said they knew they would have better health if they ate less sugar, white bread, coffee, salt, and soft drinks. They agreed they should eat more fruits, vegetables, fish, and whole grains. Eighty-five percent said they knew it was important to exercise regularly, but only 32 percent did.

During my formative years, Mother was very conscientious about our diets. As a dental assistant, and later as a teacher at the UCLA dental school, she knew that most deficiency diseases attack the gums first.

When I was studying ballet, swimming, and ice skating, as well as going to school, I ate about five good meals a day, and took vitamins.

My high-school physiology teacher told our class one day, "No one needs vitamins." I quit taking them for about a month, but began to drag a little when I usually had plenty of energy to spare. Mom casually suggested that I try the vitamins again. To my amazement, my high energy level returned.

With the Ice Follies and marriage, vitamins slowly became a thing of the past. After each of my pregnancies my health seemed to deteriorate more.

The daily mental and emotional stress of personal loneliness and unhappiness did more to deplete my body than just about anything else. I had headaches and stomachaches. My gall bladder began acting up with increasing regularity. I was tested by doctors and put on a bland diet. I gradually began eating normally, but did not regain the vitality I once had.

I was ill almost from the moment of our son's conception. For four months, I lived in a highly sedated, semiconscious state in an effort to control violent nausea.

Mike resigned from the air force during my illness because he was ordered transferred and doctors feared I would lose the baby if I were moved. I was tired much of the year following that pregnancy. When Mike junior was fifteen months old, we bought a lovely home in one of Montgomery's finest neighborhoods. In a determined effort to save money—which we didn't have anyway—I moved all of our things from our second-story apartment—in thirty-five trips! The house was large and filthy. I spent days scrubbing and scraping, making curtains, and unpacking, before I collapsed in complete exhaustion.

This time I didn't snap back after a period of rest. I spent much of the time in bed. My doctor said there didn't seem to be anything wrong, aside from the fact I had pushed myself too hard and was taking a long time to recover.

But the fatigue and nausea grew worse. I was so weak that I could barely walk. Some days I had to crawl from the sofa in the den to the bedroom, because I was too dizzy to stand up. My blood pressure was very low, but my doctor told me it was better than high blood pressure, and I would probably live longer but enjoy it less. The statement gave me little comfort at the time.

Several months passed and I had been bedridden most of the time. I entered the hospital for a battery of tests which showed I had the early symptoms of some degenerative diseases. I was kept on the bland diet and told I would have to live a fairly restricted life. A year passed; major surgery was needed and performed.

I asked my doctor about taking some vitamins to help build me up, but he said vitamins were useless. Money spent on them was like flushing it down the drain. I also asked him about giving me a five-hour glucose-tolerance

test for low blood sugar. He thought that was a fad and
was not indicated in my case. (I must say here that my
doctor is well respected and gives conscientious treatment to the best of his ability. He simply lacked knowledge in the area of nutrition—perhaps due to the fact that
it is not taught in any depth in our medical schools.)

Common sense made it evident that my body could
never get well on the diet I had been given. It was bland
and void of any nutritive value. I found a health-food
store where I could buy some natural vitamins. While I
was there, I noticed the paperback editions of Adelle
Davis's books *Let's Eat Right and Keep Fit* and *Let's
Get Well.* I had always wanted to read these books, but
felt they were outside my budget because they were
hardcover. (It seems ironic that I couldn't afford a
hardcover book but spent hundreds of dollars on medical
bills!)

From my study of those books, I devised a regimen
that I felt would meet my family's nutritional needs.
Susan was slightly hyperactive and was on medication.
She was also very small for her age. So, it appeared we
could all benefit from natural vitamins.

The results were startling. I gave myself a double dos-
age and could feel the difference within a few days.
Within three weeks, I felt better than I had in years. I
soon put myself on a diet that was recommended for
people with hypoglycemia. I limited my intake of carbohydrates and increased the amount of protein. I regained
the physical and mental energy I had once known.

The children blossomed, too. Susan grew three sizes
in one year.

I am convinced that God has given us every element to
keep our bodies strong and healthy. But if we neglect to
give our bodies the nutrients they need, we will not have
the optimum health we desire.

In all honesty, I thought my family ate very well. By
the standard of the average family, we ate much better

quality meals than most. Our children didn't have as many colds as their playmates, and had very few cavities. I restricted the use of sugar in cooking, did not make sugary desserts, and seldom had candy, soft drinks, or other sweet drinks around.

After I began studying nutrition, though, I started reading labels. If you have never been a label reader, you are in for quite a surprise!

With all my good intentions and careful shopping, there was no way our nutritional needs could be met through the processed food that was available to us. My body had been in serious need of the B-complex vitamins which had been milled out of the products we bought.

For example, when flour is bleached to a beautiful white, eighteen vitamins are stripped out of the wheat. The manufacturer can say it is "enriched" when only three vitamins are returned to the product.

Perhaps people shouldn't have to take vitamin supplements if they eat a balanced diet. But who eats a balanced diet? If we did actually eat all the foods necessary daily to provide our bodies with the nutrients we need for optimal health, would we get the necessary physical exercise to work off the calories we would consume?

Practically no one eats anything close to a balanced diet, which consists of whole grains, nuts, and seeds; several servings daily of fresh fruits and vegetables; a minimum of 60 grams of protein (ideally 75 grams) from eggs, milk, natural cheeses (not processed cheese), meat, fish, poultry, or soybeans.

Instead of giving our bodies the foods and nutrients God created for them, we are filling His holy temple with foods which are now stripped of the natural goodness they originally had. They are filled with chemical preservatives to give them long shelf life, stabilizers to keep them intact, artificial color to make them pretty, and artificial flavors to give them back the taste that was taken away when they were processed.

The soil in which these foods are grown no longer contains natural elements needed for healthy bodies. Man-made chemicals are being put into the soil to give it high yield. Poisons are sprayed on our foods to make them more resistant to insects and disease. These chemicals and poisons are taken through the root systems into the plant food itself. The waterways of the world are polluted with the chemicals used on our farms. Many are found in fish caught far out in the oceans.

Americans are overfed, but undernourished to the point where a serious national health problem exists in every age group and economic level of society. I have encountered a host of Christians who are defeated, depressed, and think they have all manner of spiritual problems, when in fact, their real problem is their diet. They are existing on cereal, white toast and jelly, coffee with sugar and artificial cream for breakfast. Midmorning slump is remedied with coffee and a cookie, or maybe a cola. Lunch is peanut butter (hydrogenated with sugar) on white bread, potato chips, and a brownie. More coffee and cola follow in the afternoon, with maybe a cupcake thrown in for good measure. Dinner is a gourmet's nightmare—even on the nights TV dinners, hot dogs, or hamburgers are not on the menu.

Tonight Mom is going to break open the three-year-old canned ham, left over from Aunt Sally's funeral. Yummy, here comes the brown sugar and sweet pineapple to give it just the right old-fashioned taste. Next, sweet-potato casserole with some more of the good brown sugar and all those cute marshmallows on top. Let's add instant whipped potatoes with gobs of margarine and a serving of peas for color. A gelatin salad with fruit cocktail would be a nice touch to go with the biscuits and jelly. For dessert, chocolate cake is always a favorite, but tonight—let's have one of those

frozen pecan pies we bought on special last week and
top it with a glob of artificial whipped cream.

Drunk on Cola?

It interests me that often the Bible discusses the problems (sin) of drunkenness and gluttony in the same
verse. Deuteronomy 21:20 says, "And they [parents]
shall say to the elders of his city, 'This son of ours is
stubborn and rebellious, he will not obey us, he is a
glutton and a drunkard.'"

> Listen, my son, and be wise,
> And direct your heart in the way.
> Do not be with heavy drinkers of wine,
> Or with gluttonous eaters of meat;
> For the heavy drinker and the glutton will
>   come to poverty,
> And drowsiness will clothe a man with rags.
> Proverbs 23:19–21

There are thousands of devoted, loving Christians
across America who would never touch a drop of alcohol
but gorge themselves in the privacy of their own kitch-
ens. With every sweet bite they are as guilty of gluttony
as the drunkard is with his wine.

There is no one on the face of the earth who loves to
eat any better than I do. I find a great delight in eating
constantly. I love to sit down at the table and stuff my
face until I am so full I can hardly move. When I was
skating, I ate five times a day—and that included several
desserts. I could put away banana splits and pie a la
mode like a veritable garbage disposal and never gain a
pound. I have never tasted a food I didn't like, and I have
come up with some pretty weird concoctions! But I can't
do that anymore. My system won't tolerate it, my body
doesn't need it, and gluttony in any form is a sin and a
substitute for Jesus Christ in my life.

Are you the product of what you eat? The quality of
your daily diet affects not only your physical well-being
but your mental attitude as well. The effects of sugar,
salt, and caffeine from cola, coffee, and tea have now
been shown to seriously hinder the efficient functioning
of the body and brain.

Outward beauty is most assuredly more than skin
deep. The way we nourish our bodies plays a most significant role in the way we look. Good looks and health
are inseparable. Look around you—the people who are
the most physically attractive are also healthy. This kind
of beauty is not always dependent on facial features or
body symmetry. Many people are attractive because
they are vibrant and well groomed. They have taken
God's gifts and made the most of them. We cannot escape the fact that their vitality and bright aliveness
comes from the care they have given their bodies.

Inner beauty comes from the workings of the Holy
Spirit within the soul of the believer. Outward beauty is
reflected through the efficient functioning of every organ
and gland under the surface of the skin. Lovely complex-
ions, shining hair, sparkling eyes, and good posture are
all the results of good nourishment.

I am most heartbroken when I look into the faces of
children. Everywhere I go, I recognize the signs of
faulty nutrition and know that they are being deprived of
the health and beauty they will some day long to have.
Babies sucking on candy, having had their taste buds
trained for sweetness from infancy when Mother put
sugar in their water. Mothers often use the excuse that
their children won't eat vegetables or fresh fruit. They
find it easier to give them what they want in preference
to what is good for their bodies.

As a Christian, everything I study forces me back to
God's Word for ultimate truth. In this age of enlighten-
ment, many believers are basking in God's grace, thinking that when He sent Jesus He repealed His laws. We

are saved by grace, but we live in obedience to the commands found in His Word. Moderate ill health to fatal disease is rampant in our country, largely because we have disregarded the promises for life and health given us in the Bible.

When God gave us the good things of the earth to be our food and sustain us, He gave us a set of dietary laws to go with it. Nowhere in the New Testament will we find these laws repealed. Most of us would never consider freely abusing the moral law, yet we may be habitually abusing the dietary laws. We reap what we sow in *every* area of our lives.

Many men of science and industry lean only on man's technology and the knowledge gained from it. The industrial and chemical revolutions of the past fifty years have brought many advances to our society, but there have also been many negative by-products. Cancer is one. The following statement comes from the *National Resources Defense Council Newsletter*, summer 1976:

> Probably the most startling revelation of all is that between 75 and 90% of all cancers are related to environmental factors. The term "environmental" in this case encompasses substances in the food we eat, and the air we breathe, and the water we drink, as well as our personal habits, occupations and lifestyles.

Throughout the world, those who live in uncivilized regions have been found to have long lifespans and are relatively free of the kinds of disease found in "civilized" areas. When our Western diets, with sugar and refined grains, have been introduced, illness has come with it. Tooth decay, cancer, and heart attacks are now common but were unheard of prior to our "improved" methods of handling and refining food.

I am not saying that every disease in America is directly attributable to the processed foods we eat; I *am* saying we have a responsibility to know what is lacking in the meals that we serve our families.

Some books are listed in the appendix to help you begin a study of how you can improve the health of your family and yourself. I implore you to educate not only yourself but also begin to educate your children and encourage others to do the same. We all like to think that Jesus is coming soon, but if He tarries we have future generations to consider whose health is at stake. It could well be survival of the fittest.

How to Start Improving Your Diet

For the past few years, I have been baking bread and other baked goods, using whole-grain flours. They are delicious and full of vitamins, protein, and minerals. I make yogurt—to be eaten plain or with fruit, blended in milk shakes, or frozen in popsicles. Cottage cheese blended with yogurt is a fine substitute for sour cream. When mixed with seasonings, it is our favorite salad dressing. We often use Parmesan or blue cheese, with a little garlic salt and Vege-sal as seasoning. It is also very good with garlic salt, Vege-sal, Italian herbs, and a spoonful of mayonnaise.

Granola can be made at home much more economically than the packaged varieties. Your imagination is your guide. Let the kids choose the ingredients. Use oatmeal, grains, shredded wheat (spoon size), wheat germ, almonds or other nuts, coconut, raisins, or other chopped, dried fruits or dates. Warm some honey and unsaturated oil together. Drizzle over the ingredients and work through the cereal with your hands. Toast the mixture in a "slow" oven, mixing periodically until it is lightly browned. Granola is not only an excellent cereal but a great snack, too.

Fresh green and yellow vegetables should be eaten at lunch and dinner. Try raw carrot and celery sticks, cucumber slices, and lettuce as part of lunch, with two cooked vegetables (steamed, still crisp) and salad with dinner. When fresh vegetables are unavailable, frozen is next best.

Fruit goes with every meal and is a wholesome between-meal snack. Each member of the family should have at least two pieces of fruit a day.

Protein—Our Body's Building Blocks

The only sources of complete protein are eggs, milk, primary-grown yeast food, cheeses, and meats (beef, lamb, chicken, turkey, and fish).

We have trillions of cells in our bodies; these cells are made of proteins. We adults ideally need to eat 60 to 75 grams of protein a day. Most of us eat less than half that amount.

Our bodies were created with the power to rebuild themselves daily as old cells wear out. This rebuilding process can only be accomplished as we supply our bodies with the required building materials it needs. In the book *How to Count Your Grams of Protein,* by Richard Talbot, an easy method for guidance is given:

Eggs   1 ounce = 3 grams (One egg is about 2 ounces.)

Milk   1 ounce = 1 gram
Cheese   1 ounce = 4 grams
Meat   1 ounce = 5 grams

The majority of us eat our greatest amount of protein at the evening meal. This is directly opposite of what will give us the greatest amount of energy for the day's activities. Breakfast is the most important meal of the day and should supply us with at least one-third and preferably one-half of our day's protein intake.

Ideally, the evening meal should be the lightest meal of the day because our body is at rest. If we will begin to readjust some of our eating habits, we can begin to experience maximum energy throughout the day.

Powdered protein is an excellent supplement to protein received from foods. We use Hoffman's Super High Protein Powder. A heaping tablespoon added to 8 ounces of milk will supply 25 grams of protein. We blend it with bananas, strawberries, cinnamon, or vanilla flavoring. A little honey and granular lecithin and torula or brewer's yeast can be added, also. This one drink is so satisfying, we do not hunger at all until lunchtime. I don't advocate the use of raw eggs, but several eggs can be cooked with milk to a soft-custard stage, kept in the refrigerator, and added to the milk shake if you wish.

The Inexpensive Rich Egg

Egg is the finest source of protein we have and is vital to a healthful diet. Lecithin, found in the yolk of an egg, is the natural emulsifier of fatty deposits in the body. If you have ever made mayonnaise you know that when the oil is slowly added to the egg it becomes suspended, evenly distributed throughout the mixture, and will not separate. This is because of the lecithin in the yolk.

The same is true as to our body chemistry. We must have a supply of lecithin, which is manufactured by our liver, in order to keep our blood vessels clean and free of fat deposits. Lecithin is also found in whole grains, nuts, and vegetable oil sold in health-food stores. Unfortunately, vegetable oil sold in supermarkets has had virtually all of its lecithin and vitamin E extracted during the processing. Increased use of eggs in feeding our families provides a comparatively inexpensive source of lecithin and protein.

The Energy Sustainer

Milk, yogurt (natural, not sugared with gelatin), cottage cheese, and natural aged cheeses also need to be a part of each day's protein intake. Processed cheese is a food of inferior quality with little significant nutritive value. These dairy products can be used in an endless variety for any meal.

The only true meat substitute is the soybean. Full fat soy flour is a wholesome, nutritious addition to baked goods. It can also be added to ground meat. Soybeans have a distinctive taste which may take some getting used to, but they are economical and many good recipes using soybeans are available. Other beans and legumes contain some incomplete protein, but they should not be considered a substitute for the foods mentioned above. Beef, lamb, fowl, and fish are excellent sources of protein and are regulars on most of our menus.

Protein gives sustained energy. Most children eat far too little protein. The grams they require are proportionate to their age. But it is better to give too much than too little.

Fats

Every nutrient is important in building and maintaining health and vitality. This includes fats. They have gained a bad reputation in recent years as being the reason for a variety of illnesses that are prevalent today.

Some fats used exclusively, or in large quantities, are harmful; other fats are necessary for good health. In an effort to lose weight or avoid fat for fear of promoting certain illnesses, many people are actually doing greater harm to their bodies than the good they seek.

It is common to think of fats only as unwanted and unneeded calories. But fats contain elements known as fatty acids, which the body requires for maximum health and efficiency. Some of the required fatty acids can be manufactured by our bodies from sugars, but three cannot. These three are called essential fatty acids—linoleic acid, arachidonic acid, and linolenic acid.

These essential fatty acids must be supplied through foods we eat. The best source available is safflower oil, preferably purchased at a health-food store. It's rather expensive, but I use it in salad dressings so that each member of the family receives a supply of fatty acids. If your budget permits, softened butter and safflower oil combined in equal parts make a great butter spread.

Fats are divided into two categories: saturated and unsaturated.

Saturated fats: These are solid or semisolid animal fats. Some vegetable fats are included.

The degree of saturation depends on the number of hydrogen atoms in the fat molecule. Saturated fats can accommodate no more hydrogen atoms. These solid fats are found in meats, cheeses, cream, egg yolks, butter, coconut, and palm oils. Both the coconut and palm oils are used in imitation cream, filled milk, margarine, and some infant formulas.

An unsaturated fat is turned into a saturated fat when hydrogen is added to it. The hydrogenation process was first begun to prevent fats and oils from becoming rancid. However, in the process of hydrogenation, the nutritive value and essential fatty acids are also destroyed. Therefore, it is wise to avoid all hydrogenated fats and foods cooked in them; specifically, canned solid vegetable fats, margarine, hydrogenated peanut butter, processed cheeses, french fries, and other deep-fried foods. Often we avoid natural cheeses, egg yolks, or butter, thinking the fat and cholesterol content are harmful; yet we eat large quantities of hydrogenated fats which are more harmful to us in the long run.

There is much concern about cholesterol these days. We hear that cholesterol adheres to the linings of blood vessels and contributes to circulatory problems, arteriosclerosis, heart attack, and stroke. With this news comes the advice to stay away from foods containing saturated fats. We then eliminate from our diets some necessary foods, perhaps without attempting to investigate the whole subject of cholesterol.

Cholesterol is not only found in saturated fats; it is also produced by the liver. If you have a normal to high intake of fatty foods and refined carbohydrates, you may obtain as much as 800 milligrams of cholesterol a day. A normal adult liver produces about 3,000 milligrams a day. Therefore, it is possible for some people to eat no foods containing cholesterol and still have a high blood-cholesterol level.

I believe the secret to all-around good health is to give our bodies all the nutrients they need. Our bodies need the protein and nutrients found in lean meats, eggs, and cheeses. If our diets are adequately balanced, we may enjoy moderate amounts of cream and butter as well, providing our cholesterol metabolism is normal.

The liver produces other fatty compounds known as triglycerides which are as harmful as cholesterol in the blood vessels. Our bodies' production of these serum fats is affected far more by the refined foods, sugar, and caffeine we eat than by a daily egg and pat of butter.

Unsaturated fats: Our bodies cannot be healthy, in fact we cannot live, without the essential fatty acids. Many common complaints are partly the result of not obtaining these essential fatty acids: hair and skin problems and some edema (water retention). Blood-sugar levels are also affected by the lack of oil in the diet.

It is a good idea to plan your family menu to include more poultry and fish, which have less saturated fat than beef and lamb. From the health-food store, buy unrefined or cold pressed oils (refrigerate after opening) and use for salad dressing, or mixed with butter. If each person has a tablespoon of safflower oil a day, the bodily need for the three essential fatty acids should be met. Soybean and corn oils also contain the three essential fatty acids, but in lesser amounts than safflower oil. For other cooking needs I use one of the bottled variety of oils found in the supermarket which contain no preservatives, but I use as little as possible. We rarely fry foods; we broil or bake most meats and fish.

Margarine is made with saturated fats, hydrogenated

oils, and chemical additives for flavor, color, and preservation. The calorie content for all fats and oils is about 100 per tablespoon. The choice between butter or margarine is which will benefit our bodily needs. My choice for moderate table use is the mixture of butter and safflower oil.

When God planned and created the foods our bodies require, He placed within them elements to both complement and counterbalance one another. No single food, like no single vitamin, can furnish all our needs. Everywhere we find a balance in nature. This balance should also be sought in planning our diets.

Carbohydrates

More myths, misunderstandings, and misinformation appear to be circulating about carbohydrates than either protein or fat. Carbohydrates are starch and sugar compounds found in nearly all foods: milk, fruits, vegetables in varying degrees, grains, seeds, and nuts.

These carbohydrates are measured by grams. We all require a certain number of grams each day for good health. The number of needed grams varies widely within individuals according to one's activities and metabolism.

Metabolism is energy production, the rate by which our bodies break down and utilize (assimilate) the foods we eat. The normal metabolism range varies widely. Two people may consume identical meals; yet one may be chubby, the other slim. Different rates of metabolism cause this. Both people may still be within the normal range.

It is even possible that the chubby one eats less. We all know many slender souls who eat enormous quantities of food and never gain weight. This is because they burn their calories at a faster rate than those of us who must eat less in order to maintain our ideal weight.

A calorie is a unit of energy-producing property in all our foods. It is common to figure our daily requirements for food according to a certain number of calories a day. This number may be determined according to age, sex, and amount of physical activity.

I have found it more helpful to calculate my body's needs according to grams of protein, carbohydrates, and fats. I could conceivably get all the calories I need each day from any one of the three sources and still be drastically deficient in many nutrients. So rather than count calories alone, we need to consider our carbohydrate, protein, and fat intake.

The average American consumes an excessive number of empty calories each day. Hundreds of grams of carbohydrates can be eaten daily from refined sugars and starches that will give the body little nutritive value. The feeling of hunger will be satisfied and a certain level of energy may be maintained; but damage to every cell and organ will be taking place when the proper and complete number of nutrients, vitamins, and minerals are consistently in short supply. Few people today suffer from a particular deficiency disease, but multitudes suffer from deficiencies of many nutrients.

Symptoms may be vague: tiredness; irritability; frequent headaches; unclear thinking; susceptibility to colds, hay fever, and flu; dry or oily skin; soft, ridged fingernails; cracked, coated, or red tongue; gum disease; decaying teeth. The list of minor complaints is almost endless.

If you voice these vague symptoms to your doctor, you will probably be told it is nerves and be given tranquilizers; or allergy and be given antihistamine; or aches and pains and be given aspirin. If you are tired, you are told to get more rest—or exercise—or just to quit worrying about it; it is all in your head. You may follow your doctor's orders to the letter and still these vague symptoms persist.

We may mask the symptoms with pills, but the root cause of the complaints is not being treated and cured. I've had all the symptoms and all the pills, but never was free of the problems until my diet was corrected.

Sadly, even when symptoms are pronounced and disease is evident, doctors rarely prescribe a diet which will provide the body with liberal amounts of every nutrient, plus supplemental vitamins and minerals.

I'm very much against processed and refined foods. I feel that if these foods are not limited or eliminated completely from our diets, we can never hope to be our best physically, mentally, and emotionally. God did not create empty calories—man did. At first it was man's desire to preserve food and later it was his desire to increase his profits. Foods may stay fresh on supermarket shelves for years, but if they won't spoil or attract bugs, there probably isn't anything left in them to feed us nutritionally, either!

No doubt you have heard comments of how, as a people, each generation is taller than the last. I have even heard it reported that this is due to the fact that our diets are greatly improved over those past generations. This is a half-truth. Yes, we are taller; that's obviously true. However, it is an error to say that it is because our diets are improved. A high intake of carbohydrates from refined sugar and flour produces rapid, increased growth of the long bones—but general muscle development, wide jaws, uncrowded teeth, vitality, and freedom from illness is not present to indicate sound health. Just because a person is tall is not an indication that he is healthy!

We need to be aware of the part that media advertising plays in our concept of "healthful" foods. May I emphatically state that commercials are designed to sell products, and are very often misleading, or completely untrue. For instance, one type of canned "fruit" drink boasts seven kinds of fruit in one 48-ounce can—with a total of 10 percent of the contents real fruit juice. Have you ever calculated that? It means that in 1½ quarts of liquid there is only a fraction more than ½ cup of these seven fruits altogether (less than 1 ounce each)! The other 43.2 ounces are a combination of water, sugar, and chemicals to flavor, color, and preserve the contents. The powdered mixes are even poorer nutritionally because they are just sugar and chemicals.

Along with milk and 100-percent natural, un-sweetened fruit juices, there is a fine drink for all ages called *water*. We would all do well to increase its use. Having a flavored drink is just a habit. If your little darling has a tantrum for her tutti-frutti-flavored drink and fudge cookie, let her cry! She will eventually get thirsty enough for water and hungry enough for an apple.

In the food department, we have a battle of the wills going on between parents and children. Unfortunately, the persistent nastiness of the kids usually wears Mom and Dad to a frazzle and they wind up giving the little dears whatever they scream for. This is not the kind of authority and training God entrusted to us as parents. These young lives are our responsibility to train and nurture. To nurture is to feed and nourish—spiritually, physically, mentally, and emotionally—all working together to develop the whole person to his full potential.

Food is so glorified in our society that it is looked upon as a reward and a show of love and affection. But proteins and fats are seldom a part of this charade.

Sweets have been elevated to the place of "the re-ward" for goodness and accomplishment. Parents, grandparents, and TV tell us, "Be good and you can have a piece of candy, a cookie, or some ice cream. If you aren't good, Mommy won't love you." So the child grows up thinking, "I deserve sweets because I am lovable and good."

Throughout life we then reward ourselves with sweets! A vicious subconscious circle becomes a vicious physical circle. Our bodies crave the sweets to elevate our blood-sugar levels, thereby giving us a "boost." When this temporary boost wears off, we grab another cola, coffee, or sweet to jack ourselves up again—and round and round we go.

I have never heard a pregnant woman say she prayed for an unhealthy child. Without exception, expectant parents say, "Nothing matters as long as the baby is healthy." Diseased millionaires have been reported as stating they would give away their fortunes in exchange for the good health they had previously enjoyed. Learning about—and practicing—good nutrition is as important to our physical bodies as feeding on God's Word is to our spiritual well-being.

When we learn to count protein and carbohydrate grams instead of just calories, we will find it much easier to keep track of the necessary amounts needed to supply our daily bodily requirements.

Blahs

Recently, when our son celebrated his birthday, he planned the day's menu. First on his list was coconut cake and ice cream; then waffles for breakfast, muffins, fried chicken, and whatever else I wanted to fill in with. My husband requested a pot of coffee and there I was wondering, should I or shouldn't I indulge with them? I did—had two waffles with honey butter, coffee, and juice for breakfast.

I baked and fixed everything in the morning; after lunch I sat down at the typewriter to work. I was sleepy and just couldn't seem to get with it.

After dinner I indulged some more—a small piece of cake and a dab of ice cream. It was delicious, but it seems absurd to feel "blah" for half a day for three minutes of tasting a plateful of junk. That can't add up to good common sense in anybody's book!

Just like any other habit which needs improvement,

eating habits can be retrained. But it is not an easy task when pictures of fabulous foods fill every magazine, and commercials blast us with every kind of edible garbage on the market. I love to cook and I have found it is just as much fun when the recipes are health building, as well as delicious. I guess it is a matter of educating our heads—brain and taste buds alike.

Your family may squeal at first when you make changes in their eating habits, but by telling them some of the things you are learning about health and the importance of good nutrition for every Christian, I think you will find they have a willingness to be their most healthy selves, too.

As you begin to discuss the subject of changes in the family eating habits, it is good to use some of the Scripture verses and explain how our bodies are the temples of God when we belong to Jesus. It can become a challenging and fun project for the whole family. God did not give us life in His image to be lived fully and abundantly as weak, sickly imitations of Jesus. God gave us everything we need to be healthy in all ways.

Food: A Weighty Subject

People approach the subject of food in two different ways—some live to eat; others eat to live.

If you have a serious weight problem, I recommend Weight Watchers, Overeaters Anonymous, or TOPS (Take Off Pounds Sensibly). The encouragement gained from groups such as these will give you the incentive to lose pounds which are keeping you from looking and feeling your best.

I have known many women who have lost enormous amounts of weight. Without exception, they have told me their entire outlook on life changed once they were happy about the way they looked. Most said they previously had a poor self-image—disliked themselves—and ate more to compensate for their dislike and frustration.

Once they shed the unwanted pounds, they began to like themselves. They enjoyed wearing attractive clothes, meeting new friends, and hearing the compliments of old friends. They realized they had been unable to experience God's best because they had substituted food for the sufficiency of Jesus to meet and conquer the problems in their lives.

Besides a more attractive figure, there are a host of other benefits to be gained from maintaining a comfortable weight. We are then giving God's temple, our body, the care it deserves.

When a person overeats, considerable stress is placed on every organ. The body must work harder to digest and assimilate large quantities of food. This also increases strain on the heart and muscles. Extreme overweight makes exercising difficult and even impossible in some cases. The life span of the overweight person is shortened by several years, and the incidence of illness and stress diseases is measurably increased. In short, we really miss a lot of the enjoyment of being alive.

A few weeks ago, I had lunch with a friend who is currently attending meetings of a local Overeaters Anonymous group. She shared how it had taken her a long time to recognize fully how her love of food has not only burdened her but affected others as well. She has a small granddaughter who is the delight of her life. They have a wonderfully close relationship, and bear a striking resemblance to one another in looks, mannerisms, likes and dislikes.

One day as they were talking, the little girl was admiring a lovely pin on her grandmother's dress. When told that someday it would belong to her, she looked sadly at her grandmother and said, "I do love it, but, Grandma, will I have to be fat to wear it?"

Within that child was the fear that being like grandmother meant being fat. That single comment gave my friend the determination to become the best example of a Christian woman and grandmother.

If you share this "weighty" problem, determine today to:

1. Confess it: The Bible says gluttony is a sin.
2. Ask Jesus: to give you help to discipline your eating habits.
3. Question: With every bite ask yourself if you need it or would it do the garbage disposal more good.
4. Write: Keep a written list of everything you eat—what and how much. Most overeaters are unaware of both the frequency of eating and the amounts consumed between meals.
5. Join: a group whose goals match yours. You will find friendship and encouragement with others who share your problem. It will also be another opportunity to be a witness for Jesus.

Vitamins: To Take or Not to Take

Two reasons for taking natural vitamin supplements stand out in my mind. With automation and the convenient household gadgets we enjoy today, most people do not do enough physical labor to burn up each day's supply of carbohydrates. Also, there is no guarantee that the foods we buy contain the nutrients we need. Soils are demineralized and loaded with chemicals. Fruits and vegetables are picked before they are fully ripe. Vitamin loss is extensive during processing. Exposure to light and oxygen destroys vitamins, and our fresh vegetables are days away from the garden by the time we eat them.

I am neither a health-food faddist nor a vitamin fanatic. I am a Christian who believes that the best health throughout life will be obtained if we adhere as nearly as possible to the natural foods God has given us. God gave mankind intellect and creative ability. This creativity has given us untold benefits, but there is almost always a price to pay for progress. We are paying that price in our health and well-being.

I have personally experienced the difference between

good and poor health. I would like to maintain and hopefully better the health I enjoy today. I don't advocate large quantities of vitamins, but I do believe that a well-rounded program is most beneficial.

The chemical properties of synthetic vitamins equal natural vitamins, but there is one difference which causes me to prefer natural sources. In a natural source, related elements are present. There are about forty nutrients which are known to be needed by our bodies, and I believe that others will be discovered in the future.

The cost of natural vitamins varies considerably. The most expensive brand is not necessarily the best brand. Some vitamins available through independent dealers are several times more expensive than my brand but, after examining these supplements, I would not recommend them at all. On the other hand, there are vitamins available at considerably lower prices than the norm. I have investigated some of these and feel their quality may match the price.

Before I selected the brands and amounts I felt suited our family's needs, I did a great deal of reading and planned what I felt was adequate. We take:

B complex with C—Three brands have almost identical composition and balance: Plus Products Formula 72, Thompson, and Solgar.
A and D—5,000 and 400 units each
E—100 units, D-ALPHA in mixed tocopherols, for the children
400 units of same for adults
Multi-Mineral tablets by Plus Products
C—From rose hips with bioflavonoids
Alfalfa tablets

I keep extra calcium-magnesium tablets, pantothenic acid, zinc, PABA, iron, and B6 tablets for occasional use. There are some good multivitamin and mineral tablets on the market that give just about everything I take in one tablet. When traveling, I use one of these—either Plus Products Formula 74 or Solgar's Naturvite.

A rich natural source of B vitamins, many minerals, and excellent protein is brewer's or primary-grown torula yeast. One to two tablespoons a day mixed with milk or juice will provide all the B vitamins most people need. Two tablespoons also provides about 16 grams of protein. I use Plus Products Formula 250. It is torula food yeast and has a milder taste than brewer's yeast. Some people enjoy the flavor of yeast, but I would never go so far as to state that it tastes good! I mix it with milk or tomato juice, drink it fast, and have a water chaser handy! It is a midafternoon pick-me-up par excellence.

I know scores of people whose diets were quite adequate and whose only improvement was the daily addition of yeast. They immediately experienced a greater sense of well-being. If you do nothing else but eliminate sweets and add yeast, I think you will be doing yourself a favor.

What to Avoid

I believe much of the irritability, nervousness, headaches, and fatigue experienced by millions of people daily could be eliminated if they would restrict their daily caffeine intake. Caffeine is an alkaloid having addictive as well as stimulating properties. It plays havoc with the blood-sugar level and affects every part of the body. Decaffeinated coffee should only be used in moderation, however, because potentially harmful chemicals are used in extracting the caffeine.

If tea is steeped less than two minutes, its caffeine content is low. After two minutes, it soars tremendously.

There really isn't anything good to say about soft drinks—and colas are the worst. Drop a tooth (one the good fairy left behind) or a nail in the leading brand of cola, and leave it for a few days. This is potent stuff! I firmly believe that if the national corporations weren't so huge and powerful, this stuff could have long ago been banned.

Did you know that oxalic acid in chocolate destroys calcium in milk? Chocolate milk is yummy—but bad for the tummy!

White flour is great for making an inexpensive paste for the kids to play with, good for making papier-mâché, even for hanging wallpaper. Just don't eat it! Bread may be the staff of life, but *that* bread bore no resemblance to the white, fluffy stuff we have today.

Mother used to dip my hair ribbons in a sugar-water solution to renew the crispness. That's a good use for sugar. At the moment I am hard pressed to think of another good use for it. Sugar is probably the greatest single health hazard in the United States today.

Yogurt

Yogurt has been a food staple for centuries and is an excellent addition to every diet. Many companies have jumped on the yogurt bandwagon and are marketing imitations of the natural variety. They have added gelatin, sugar, preservatives, flavoring, and coloring and have come up with a pretty tasty concoction. But wholesome, nutritious yogurt it is not!

Yogurt makers, available in stores, are not expensive, and make the best yogurt. Yogurt can also be made without a maker, but the temperature must be watched carefully. Here is a receipe: Blend 2 cups powdered skim milk with 4 cups water. Scald and let cool until just warm. Mix ½ can evaporated milk a little at a time with ½ cup Dannon plain yogurt, add to warm milk. Place in glass jars in pan of warm water up to within one inch of the rim; cover and keep at 105 degrees to 120 degrees for four hours until a firm, custardlike consistency is achieved. Refrigerate.

Use in salad dressings, topped with fruit or orange-juice concentrate, or sprinkled with toasted wheat germ.

The bacteria which cultures yogurt and buttermilk is the same valuable bacteria found in the intestine. When generous amounts are present, this bacteria synthesizes B vitamins in the intestine.

Hyperactivity and Learning Disabilities in Children

The problem of hyperactivity in children is rapidly growing in the United States. Thankfully, tremendous strides have been made in finding the cause. It is now a well-established fact that most hyperactivity and minimal learning disabilities in children can be traced to inferior diets. Their systems cannot tolerate chemical additives, food coloring, and copious amounts of sugar. When put on corrective diets of natural foods in which no chemical preservatives, additives, colors, or flavorings are present, they often show improvement almost overnight.

These children know they have a problem. They dislike their actions but have no control over their activity and behavior. When good behavior is attained through diet, they are happy to stick to their diets; they like the results.

I know the trauma and turmoil this kind of child produces within himself and his family. One of our children experienced five years of the effects of hyperactivity. All of the drugs which were being prescribed at that time were tried. The overall effect was awful. The drugs masked the symptoms but did not touch the root cause. This lovely child was forced to live a very unpleasant life in many respects, because of her inability to be quiet and learn.

When Susan was ten, we found, to our overwhelming gratitude, that she was a poor reader because she had a cross dominance between her eye and hand coordination. She is right-handed and had a dominant left eye. Somehow she was unable to see the middle letters of words with more than one or two syllables. Daily exercises increased her reading to her own grade level in a short time.

After much prayer, we also found a doctor who considered nutrition a valuable part of overall treatment. I had been giving Susan natural vitamins, but we found that she had an unusually high requirement for B6 and magnesium. With the addition of these supplements, her irritability and uncontrolled activity ceased. Unable to believe our eyes, we experimented to see if the vitamins had really made the difference. When she was off the B6 and magnesium for two days, the hyperactivity reappeared, along with irritability and highly emotional responses. When the vitamins were resumed, she relaxed and was cheerful.

Her school grades have steadily improved over the years. She is now a beautiful teenager and a cheerleader in high school.

If you have a child with any kind of physical or learning disability, I urge you to read the books listed in the appendix. Seek guidance and the help of a doctor trained to give nutritional advice and vitamin therapy. There is more at stake than physical help alone. If left untreated, these children can suffer needless mental anguish which can have long-lasting effects.

Are Nutritious Foods More Expensive?

I am regularly asked, "Can I afford to feed my family these foods? Aren't they terribly expensive?"

My response is, "You can't afford not to. Ill health is much costlier than good health."

I believe I spend considerably less than most families and we eat twice as well. I shop specials. I keep my freezer filled and store staples, which I purchase in quantity, in an extra cabinet in the basement. I enjoy home canning and freeze fresh summer fruits and vegetables. This also saves money.

Home-baked bread is half the price of the supermarket

varieties. We make whole wheat and rye for daily use. Delicious rolls, muffins, and coffee cakes can be made in quantity and frozen for later use.

I use a lot of powdered skim milk in cooking and some of us prefer it for drinking. That saves a bit on the overall milk bill.

Fresh fruit, fresh and frozen vegetables, and cheeses are expensive but affordable when less money is spent on convenience foods.

When we eat wholesome, nourishing foods our body needs less quantity. Our energy level remains high when protein is adequate; there is no craving for sweets.

Also, with wholesome foods, it is easier to maintain a proper weight. It is a fact that when our hunger is satisfied, we don't overeat.

Physical beauty *is* more than skin deep. Inner beauty shines through every Christ-controlled child of God. The health and radiance which come from partaking of the good things of the earth are also reflected through the life and well being of His children. Good nutrition is vital for every believer who wishes to experience God's best for his life.

10

Best Foot Forward

The care we give to our outward appearance is a demonstration of our relationship with Christ. During the Puritan and Victorian eras, it was considered sinful for a Christian to be fashionably dressed. Somehow, if one possessed any godly virtues, they were immediately recognizable by the clothes one wore!

Unfortunately, many of these notions remain today. I have heard many people say they are not interested in hearing about Christianity because to be a Christian one has to be straitlaced, somber, and sad. They feel that being a Christian means giving up everything enjoyable and attractive in life.

Scripture can so easily and convincingly be taken out of context. This has frequently happened in the case of 1 Peter 3:3. I do not feel this verse forbids careful grooming or attractive attire. The verse shows that true beauty comes from within. Outward adornment for the sake of appearance *alone*—to draw attention to oneself—is wrong.

Whether male or female, we are to reflect the image of Christ in every area of life. This includes our outer appearance.

The woman in Proverbs 31:10–31 was considered an excellent wife whose worth was priceless. She was dynamic, intelligent, industrious, compassionate, and well groomed. In the Hebrew text, each letter of the Hebrew alphabet is used to begin each of the twenty-two verses—as if to say her life and activities went from A to Z. Godliness is seen in the physical, mental, and emotional, as well as the spiritual, realm of life.

In order to gain understanding of 1 Peter 3:1–4 in the original language, I called a professor of Greek at Trinity Evangelical Divinity School. I was delightfully surprised that the interpretation reinforced my personal feelings about the whole scope of grooming. The various Greek words are most interesting and deal with far more than clothing. The passage encompasses our whole demeanor, referring to outward deportment (self-control versus reckless behavior); physical bearing (good posture); sensitivity to interpersonal relationships; right thinking; being well organized; good taste in respectable, well-arranged clothing; good judgment and common sense; inconspicuousness, modesty, and respect. In the following paragraphs I will develop some of these implications and will discuss how to apply what I believe will honor God through careful grooming.

A Christian should not live in a dream world, divorced from reality. We live in and should be in touch with the real world. According to Scripture, we are "the light of the world" (Matthew 5:14). We are to take an active part in the world, but because of Jesus we do not have to be conformed to its ways, by partaking of the practices of ungodly people.

Do Clothes Make the Person?

The Christian who is seeking God's best should strive to be well organized. Some people have the natural ability to be better organized than others. Those without the natural ability can train themselves to be better organized.

Jesus did not set an example of haphazard living. In His humanity, there was a goal and a purpose in life. As Christians, we should develop goals and a distinct purpose for living. These goals cannot become a reality for the person who remains disorganized.

Organization comes first within the mind and then is borne out through one's actions and appearance. For instance, if a person is mentally disorganized, his clothing is likely to be sloppy and as mismatched as his thoughts. An efficient, well-organized person will reflect that mind-set in careful grooming. The following examples illustrate how clothing can be determined by mental attitudes.

First, let's examine the disheveled-looking person: education, training, and exposure to life may or may not be a factor in this person's unkempt looks. His clothes may be mismatched, soiled, unpressed, shoes not shined, hair a mess, because he has disorganized thinking and habit patterns, poor self-image, or no childhood training. Poor work habits at home or on the job often reflect his disorganized thinking.

Do you know anyone who is a flamboyant dresser? Often this person is seeking recognition from others. He is probably quite self-centered and has fairly shallow interests in life. At first sight, I tend to think this type of person is not a Christian, but I have been proven wrong!

If the clothing is suggestive, tending to draw one's attention for sensual purposes, the person's actions will usually be as overt as the clothes.

But we all know at least one individual who is neat, clean, and pressed, wearing classically tailored clothes. This person's dress reflects a well-organized mind.

We are not to draw attention to ourselves, either through actions or dress. As Christians, we naturally desire to draw others to Christ. If our appearance is sloppy, flamboyant, or sensual, we will draw attention to ourselves. If our clothing is neat, well coordinated, and in good taste, we can feel confident about our attractive appearance, but not detract from the real beauty which is Christ in us.

First Peter 3:3 contrasts inner beauty with overt (showy) clothing. The inference is that we should develop good—even elegant—taste in clothing and grooming. But one cannot help but pity the poor person known only for his clothing, jewels, or physical features. As Christians, we want to develop the whole person.

When we speak of good taste in clothing, fine tailoring,

simple design, or elegance, sometimes people automatically think that must mean expensive! This is not necessarily true.

Personally, I would rather have one or two good dresses—purchased on sale at 50 percent off!—than a closet full of inexpensive clothes. A garment of good quality and simple, tailored design keeps it style and wearability longer than one styled after changing current trends.

Through wise shopping, most people can afford a nice outfit or two a year. I have always had expensive taste and a limited pocketbook, so *clearance* is my favorite word!

For several years I sewed most of my clothes. Mother made many of my dresses when I was growing up. We would go to the expensive shops and look at the clothes. Sometimes I would sketch a design or two on paper. Then we would go to J. C. Penney's basement and buy material which was often almost identical to the expensive clothes. I was one of the best-dressed girls in school and no one knew that my clothes were homemade.

When I learned to sew, I would copy expensive designs from shops or magazines. I'd make a pattern or use pieces from several patterns and make a sample garment out of muslin. Sewing is a very creative outlet. And with the machines, easy patterns, and lessons available today, anyone can learn to sew.

If you decide a "new you" is in order, I hope the following suggestions will help. Some people have a flair for fashion and some don't. If you recognize that your talents are in places other than fashion coordination, don't be shy about seeking advice. Most people who have the natural talent are happy to give helpful advice. As Christians, I think there is a real joy in being able to share our talents and abilities with others. We need not feel awkward about asking someone else to help us be our best.

Many people don't know how attractive they can be because they have never taken advantage of some of the opportunities to learn good-grooming techniques. Those articles where someone is "redone" from head to toe always fascinate me. The change is so remarkable and the comments are invariably, "I didn't know I could look so good!"

For Ladies Only

I know the suggestions I am making are most elementary, but bear with me because what may not apply to you may be the very thing another reader needs. I like to see a woman develop an individual sense of style. Wear what looks good—even if it isn't what the Paris designers are showing this season! Few of us have the time, money, or desire to look as though we just stepped out of *Vogue* magazine. If we did, we would probably be carrying the fashion bit to an unwise extreme.

The opposite extreme is to hold on to a style that is so outdated it looks completely ridiculous. As is true everywhere in our Christian lives, balance and harmony are in order.

Some women feel they have overcome the problem of varying skirt lengths by wearing only slacks and pantsuits. I enjoy slacks and feel there is wonderful comfort and freedom in wearing them, but not all the time! If there is one thing I would most like to see, it is more women in good-looking dresses and skirts. I don't think a women in pants ever looks as feminine as a lady in a lovely dress.

One day a few years ago, I tried a little experiment and had such fun. Mike invited me downtown for lunch and I dressed up in one of my best outfits. I had noticed a man would seldom open a door for me or step aside to let me get on an elevator first when I was wearing slacks. In general, men were no longer extending the little courtesies which put them in the gentleman class.

So, this day I decided to see if they reacted differently when I looked like the lady I am. I had a long list of errands, which began at the post office. The postal clerk did a double take when I came to the counter and cheerfully said, "Good morning, how are you today?" He straightened up to his full height and was so nice I couldn't help but be a bit amused. As I walked to the door, another man quickly opened it and nodded as I said, "Oh, thank you, sir." The whole day was that way—smiles, nods, opened doors, and almost-forgotten kindnesses and courtesies which added up to a very pleasant day.

These little things foster respect and appreciation between men and women. I know it is popular today to say, "Well, I am perfectly capable of opening my own doors." Of course you are—who can deny it?—but that's not the point at all. It is the enjoyment and recognition of the niceties of life.

When I walked into my husband's office, his eyes lit up and he said, "Wow, you look beautiful. I'll be the envy of every man in the place!" Several times that day he showed his appreciation for the bit of extra effort I had taken to look like a lady. All in all, it was a marvelous day and I determined then to put those skirts on regularly. That included wearing them around the house a few times a week, too.

It is very easy to slip into the habit of wearing a uniform at home. For years I wore slacks, tennis shoes, and a UCLA sweat shirt most of the time. It's great! You can do anything in an outfit such as that—jog, clean, play with the kids, run errands, work in the yard. One day Mike said, "I never know if you are coming or going to exercise class."

Another time when our son was little, he looked at my face, which had no makeup on it, and asked, "Oh, Mama, what's the matter with your face?"

I replied, "Honey, that's the real me."

He looked at me seriously and said, "I like you better with the rosy in your cheeks."

You know, we all look better when we have a little rosy in our cheeks.

I *feel* better when I know I look my best. My family appreciates it and others seem to notice, too. Most important, God knows I want to be my best as a witness for Him; that's an unbeatable combination.

If you haven't been buying dresses lately and wish to begin planning a wardrobe, you will naturally want to make the best use of your (God's) money. Choose garments which can be mixed and matched with other things. Two or three outfits can be switched around to make six. Many fabrics today can be worn nearly all year round. Blouses, sweaters, and accessories change the basics completely.

Select shoes and a nice purse in a basic dark color which you like—navy, brown, or black. Then build the coordinating colors from that. Ask a saleslady for help in putting a complete outfit together.

I see many women today who don't seem to buy or sew according to their correct size. If you are a size 16, buy a size 16 and shy away from those lightweight polyesters. They show every dimple! I enjoy wearing panty hose as much as anyone, but there are clothes which require good old-fashioned undergarments to get the smooth, sleek line that makes us and the dress look superb. Knits are easy to care for and have many desirable features, but fabrics which have been blended with natural fibers have more body and hold a better line— especially for sizes over nine.

Color does a great deal to enhance or detract from one's appearance. Most women look their loveliest in soft colors best suited to their skin tone and hair color. Artificial lights can play tricks with colors. Often only daylight will tell you if a particular shade is for you.

Blush, lipstick, and eye-shadow colors can also vary

according to the colors you are wearing, as well as your skin tone and hair color. At the cosmetic counters in better stores the ladies have been trained in beauty care. Ask for their suggestions. I am not convinced that expensive cosmetics have any more to offer than their well-known names. I have always had fine results with moderately priced cosmetics. My skin is fair and tender. I am pleased with Almay hypoallergenic products.

Beautiful skin is a matter of heredity, nutrition, and proper care. A daily cleansing, toning, and moisturizing routine is a must. Surprisingly, many women neglect the precautionary measures of very clean skin. I recommend cleansing twice daily with a mild facial soap or cream.

Toning is done with lotions of varying astringency strengths. This freshens and stimulates the face and removes the last traces of cleanser and makeup. A strong astringent which contains alcohol to cut the oil works best on oily skin. Dry skin needs a mild astringent which freshens without alcohol and tones very gently.

As skin ages it becomes dryer. A moisturizer acts as a protective barrier between your skin and the world, holding in moisture. Many fine products are available. We use Mennen Baby Magic and Oil of Olay. But, without makeup, most women look sickly. A light touch usually achieves the finest results.

For daytime, a cover stick to match your skin tone may be all the foundation you need to lighten the circles under your eyes or cover any discolorations on your face. Blush, a little mascara, eyebrow pencil, and lipstick should round out your daytime makeup nicely. Always try to match the light in which you apply your makeup to the light in which you will be seen. If daytime makeup is applied by artificial light, you will probably put on too much color for daytime wear.

For evening or special daytime outings, a light foundation makeup with a little more accent on the eyes may be added. Go easy on the eye shadow and false eyelashes. It is easy to look theatrical and overdone. Eye shadow should never be so vivid that one sees a splash of blue or green immediately upon looking at you. Muted, delicate shades will enhance your eyes, one of your most expressive features.

A new hairstyle can really boost a woman's morale. Your haircut should fit your total image—bone structure, hair type and color, height, weight, and even the condition of your skin.

I would adore having a hairstyle which only required a shampoo and shake of my head to have it fall in place. When I tried it, I looked like Dracula's sister. It just is not what suits my face the best.

In choosing a hairstyle, one's life-style must also be considered. A bouffant hairdo piled high on the head may be lovely with a formal gown at the ball, but with a polyester pantsuit it's a bit out of place! The same is true for the short, boyish cuts. They may be great for the tennis courts, but are not very feminine with a dress or suit. A permanent or body wave can make a soft, feminine style easy for any woman to handle.

If your time and budget allows a weekly trip to the beauty shop, your operator will enjoy experimenting with a new style. I have never gone to the beauty salon regularly. I have my hair cut professionally twice a year. I give myself permanents and trim my hair in between cuts. With all the new home equipment, anyone can learn to care for her hair with a little practice.

When Mike and I were first married, there were no electric curlers. My fine hair had to be pincurled every night. I tied a red cotton handkerchief around my head to hold my curls in place. Add to that vision of loveliness a long, flannel nightgown and bootees and you have a mental picture of me as a young woman ready for bed. The same outfit night after night left much to be desired, to say the least.

We should even be attractive when we are ready for

bed. A satin pillowcase eliminates the need for headgear to keep the hair set from being ruined. Hot rollers in the morning give a quick touch-up if needed. Two or three pretty nightgowns are worth every penny. Chances are your husband will give you a blank check if you tell him what you want to buy! Just before bedtime, apply a light film of moisturizer (no goopy creams), and don't forget a touch of lip gloss and cologne. They improve the complexion of your marriage.

As we consider our looks from head to toe, a few words about nail care should be added. If your skin is dry or sensitive to detergents, you may need to wear rubber gloves when working in water. Many excellent biodegradable products are gentle on the hands and tough on dirt. It is always a good idea to keep a dispenser of hand lotion at the kitchen sink, to use after doing the dishes. Be sure to massage the lotion in around the cuticles.

Once a week use a good cuticle remover. Apply the remover to cuticles softened from a bath or from doing the dishes. A few minutes later, gently brush around the cuticle. (I use an old, soft toothbrush.) Follow the cuticle treatment with filing to reshape and smooth the nails.

Applying an undercoat, two coats of polish, and a top coat will help your manicure last the entire week. The less expensive brands of polish may not last, but Revlon or a comparably priced polish will hold up through the week. I wear polish, do not use rubber gloves, and my manicure stays nice for many days.

No regular beauty routine need take a lot of time. The few extra minutes spent bring wonderful rewards. You feel good when you look good. When I look tacky, I feel tacky, and get less done during the day. For years I seemed to have the unconscious thought that if I wore earrings the vacuum cleaner wouldn't run! Now I know I can do my work in a blouse, a skirt, and even earrings and a necklace. It is nice not to have to run and hide when the doorbell rings or apologize for the way you look. Invest in a couple of cute aprons to protect your clothes.

During the fifteen years I had preschoolers at home, there was considerably more housework to do than after they were all in school. In those early years I got locked into wearing the "uniforms" I mentioned earlier. I guess I thought I had to look like a charwoman in order to be effective. Whatever the reason, it *is* possible to break the uniform habit, even with small children at home. Here's the way I did it.

When I got up, I'd fix my hair and put on some makeup and an attractive robe for breakfast. After Mike left for the office, I'd put on my working duds and dig in. The children's afternoon nap time was my leisure time most days. I liked to soak in the tub and read, or shower and have time for some uninterrupted project. When the children were too old to sleep, they still had a "nap time" with quiet play in their rooms. With my hard work finished, I looked forward to putting on fresh, more attractive clothes. I fixed my hair and face again, too. This routine worked wonderfully for me, and might work for you.

One time a reporter from the *New York Times* came to a city where I was giving a seminar. She was to interview me for a feature in the Sunday magazine section. She was young, single, very liberated, and just plain dirty. Her hair was uncombed, clothes wrinkled and ill fitting, with dirty toes sticking out of her sandals. I wondered how she could possibly relate to anything I said about maintaining a happy, well-balanced marriage and family life. (The article later proved she couldn't relate to any of it!)

As the reporter and I talked privately at dinner before the seminar, one of the first questions she asked was if I always looked so well groomed. I told her that I tried to be, whenever I could. She expressed the thought that in marriage, shouldn't you be able to be yourself? I explained my feelings about grooming to her in this way: "To me, being 'yourself' doesn't mean being sloppy. I like to be my best at home because I love my family and wish to be an example of Christian womanhood for my children. My husband likes to come home in the evening to an attractive, well-groomed wife. When we were dating, I always looked nice; why shouldn't I look as nice now that we are married? *I* also like to look good."

I went on to tell her that Mike has seen me at my worst. He has mopped my brow after surgery; he has cared for me when I was ill; been my shoulder to cry on when we have lost a loved one or suffered other hurts. Through the years we have gone through many hard times together. When the house burned, we fought the fire together; I didn't look so well groomed covered with soot. When it was over we collapsed on the floor together, laughing at the way we looked, and said, "Whew, I'm glad that's over!"

Sure he's seen me at my worst, but it doesn't have to be that way every day. Whenever I can, I want to put my best foot forward for my Lord and for others.

For Men Only

I must confess, I feel a bit out of my element in writing about grooming for men. Mike and I were married in 1954, so I have observed a neat, well-groomed husband for many years. Let me assure you the suggestions I make come with his approval.

Whether you wear a business suit, uniform, or work clothes, each of you is an ambassador for Jesus Christ in your chosen line of work. We are His representatives everywhere we go.

And don't think women don't notice! The first thing I notice about a man are good manners, neatness, and cleanliness, in that order. We are blessed with a fine plumber who is a gentleman in every sense of the word. When he comes late in the day, he is far from neat and clean; but he is always thoughtful, courteous, and careful not to leave a mess when he leaves. He rates high on my list!

He says he looks forward to that hot shower and clean clothes when he gets home. It is so easy to come home after a hard day's work and flop in a chair still wearing greasy, dirty clothes, instead of cleaning up for the most important people in the world—your family.

Many men who are in suits all day like to come home and get into old, rumpled clothes to flop around in. Their families rarely have the chance to see them look nice. How often our families see only the side of our lives that we are so careful to shield from the rest of the world! I'm not advocating Brooks Brothers suits for at-home wear, but I think we need to reach a happy medium between the extremes seen in the comedy show "The Odd Couple."

As a wife, let me say how disconcerting it is to be dressed in fresh clothes, set a nice table, and prepare a lovely dinner which must be served to a group of grubbies! Children are great imitators and learn more from what we do than from what we say. It is good training for them to see the leader set the example of what it means to be a gentleman in his home. Children's behavior and manners improve when the family sits down together looking clean and tidy.

The old duds are fine for working on the car or around the house and yard, but look at it this way—you don't want your wife to go to the supermarket with rollers in her hair; there's a time and place for everything. Some sights are welcome; others aren't.

There is a very worthwhile book called *Dress for Success* by John T. Molloy. He is an expert in the field of grooming and works in an advisory capacity with many corporations.

He says it is common for a man to be turned down for a position because of the way he looks. One may even have better qualifications, but if he looks "seedy," the sharp, well-dressed guy will get the job. Whether it appeals to you or not, appearances do count.

A new kind of conservatism is emerging once again in men's clothing. It is a welcome sight to me after some of the mod-type suits and sport clothes of the late sixties and early seventies. It's coats and ties, gentlemen— preferably a coat that matches your trousers and vest, in dark blue, gray, or beige.

It's no bargain to save on initial expenditures if clothes don't wear well. Always purchase clothes which have synthetic fibers mixed with pure wools or cottons. Nothing looks worse than the pure polyester shine and pucker. When you buy clothes, insist that they be fitted properly. Trousers should be long enough so your socks don't show when you walk, but not so long that they break too much or touch the ground. A salesman who has been in the men's clothing business for a while can usually give good advice.

Shirts which are polyester-cotton blends are easier to care for. However, some men find them too uncomfortable and must buy 100 percent cotton shirts. Here, it is really a matter of individual preference. For business wear, the only acceptable colors are white, palest blue, gray, beige, yellow, or pinstripe. Everything else falls into the sport-clothes class.

The key to making a wardrobe work well is color coordination, beginning with two basic colors which are compatible. Pattern, except in ties, should be so subtle that there is merely a hint of it in order to allow for easy mixing. No bold plaids, please!

According to John Molloy, "Whether you like it or not, or believe it or not, your tie, more than any other aspect of your appearance, will determine how I and other people view your status, credibility, personality and ability." It appears the selection of the right tie is as important as the suit you wear with it! Generally, men should select their own ties. The best ties are made of silk or a combination of silk and polyester. The weight of the lining material is also important because this often determines how well the tie will hold a knot.

Tie patterns in order of preference are solid colors, polka dots, evenly repeating patterns, diagonal stripes, ivy league, and paisley prints. If your ties don't fit the list, it's time to treat yourself to some new ones.

It won't do any good to put a great wardrobe together if you don't take care of it. If your suit is thrown over a chair when you get home, the next time you wear it it will look as though it's been thrown over a chair! Use pants hangers, so the trousers can hang straight while in the closet. Wooden suit hangers help coats maintain the proper shape.

Mike always puts shoe trees in his shoes when he takes them off and claims it adds twice as much wear to the shoes. He also polishes his shoes each morning and that polishes the entire outfit. I have observed many men who were well dressed except for their shoes. It spoiled their looks completely.

May I squeeze in a comment here about socks? Pastel or brightly colored socks may be sold in some stores, but that doesn't mean you have to buy them! Likewise, short athletic socks are fine for jogging and working out, but that's as far as they go.

Black, brown, or navy over-the-calf socks should be worn the rest of the time. A pair of white knee-length socks look best in the summer with a white or light blue suit; otherwise stick with the dark colors. Notice the emphasis on over-the-calf or knee lengths. The image of a well-groomed man is destroyed when he sits down and exposes a hairy leg.

I must admit I heaved a sigh of relief when I recently read that leisure suits were out. Nothing looked so dreadful on so many as polyester leisure suits. Wallets bulged out of back pockets, tummies bulged over trousers and out the front of jackets. Every spot and snag showed. Rolled-back cuffs and gold necklaces look lovely on the ladies, but men just don't look like men (to me) when they are walking jewelry ads.

Sport clothes and jackets are made for casual wear, but are seldom welcomed at a business or professional firm, says Mr. Molloy. He claims a plaid sport coat says, "I'm here to play and not to work."

Regarding Children

It is our responsibility as parents to teach good grooming to our children. If some kids will only take a bath when they are personally ushered into the shower, it's up to Mom or Dad to do the ushering.

Every day I must remind our son to wash his face and hands and comb his hair before coming to the dinner table. I expect I may have to tell him that as long as he is in our care.

I think it is a big mistake to let kids make all the rules. Children must be taught respect for authority as well as neatness, cleanliness, and good manners. And these things are best learned at home. It is up to us parents to monitor what our children wear. If a young person is allowed to run around dirty, in cruddy clothes, with hair that resembles a huge Brillo pad, his actions and attitudes will reflect the kind of permissiveness which is being built into kids through parental neglect.

Our beautiful Christian young people have every opportunity to reach their full potential in life when we parents are dedicated to showing them the way.

Heredity, nutrition, and careful grooming are essential ingredients for the spiritual and physical well-being of every member of God's family.

11

Making Harmony Your Goal

Within every person are hopes for the future, dreams and goals to be fulfilled. Harmony is achieved in our lives as we learn to sort through our priorities and plan for what we believe is God's will for us. Happiness and a gentle, calm spirit come as the result of our yielding to Christ and our adaptability to the surprises of each new day.

When the source of grooming was explained as first beginning in the mind and soul of the believer, I said it came through organized thinking. Our mental habits and attitudes are evidenced in every area of our lives. When we wish to bring God's gifts together in our lives everything needs to be considered: finances, physical fitness, and how we relate to others.

In working to improve the quality of our lives, it isn't a rigid kind of ABC routine. Life should be flexible and workable to include those things which are most important. We must also realize that many goals and dreams will be unfulfilled. This is often the normal result of changing situations as the years go by. Yet wonderful satisfaction comes from developing and pursuing the goals and directives for Christian living found in God's Word.

No two people are the same; each of us has different goals. But our ultimate goal is the same—to bring honor and glory to our Lord Jesus.

Goals come in two categories: short-range goals and long-range goals. Short-range goals involve planning for immediate needs. Long-range goals take us as far into the future as our minds can envision.

One day Mike was near a school for the blind and watched as a group of students was being instructed in how to learn their way around the city. This day they were given one long-range goal and some short-range goals. The long-range goal was to go four blocks around a set course which would bring them back to the school. The short-range goals were to break the long-range goal into steps which could easily be conquered. Even the shortest distances covered were goals attained—steps through crowded sidewalks, curbs, and streets. Finally, one day, they would be confident enough to move freely through the busy Chicago streets.

Life is this way. We learn to move through each day one step at a time, in order to make it possible to accomplish our greater purposes in life.

The Bible is full of verses which tell us that wise men make plans. It is not stepping out of God's direction to plan for the future. God gave us intelligence, experience, and instruction to use in building our lives.

Proverbs gives us an abundance of information on the right way to live. Proverbs 16:1–9 is just one of many passages:

The plans of the heart belong to man,
But the answer of the tongue is from the Lord.
All the ways of a man are clean in his own sight,
But the Lord weighs the motives.
Commit your works to the Lord,
And your plans will be established.
The Lord has made everything for its own purpose,
Even the wicked for the day of evil.
Everyone who is proud in heart is an abomination to
    the Lord;
Assuredly, he will not be unpunished.
By lovingkindness and truth iniquity is atoned for,
And by the fear of the Lord one keeps away from
    evil.
When a man's ways are pleasing to the Lord,
He makes even his enemies to be at peace with him.
Better is a little with righteousness
Than great income with injustice.
The mind of man plans his way,
But the Lord directs his steps.

For several years, Mike and I lived without common goals for our marriage and family life. We had never taken the time to sit down together and talk about what we hoped to accomplish in these areas. We did not freely discuss individual needs and how we could meet those needs.

Harmony in the home comes through the sharing of needs, responsibilities, and interests of each member of the family. In the rush of today's world, we don't take time to listen to one another. It takes time to plan and to care about what is important to someone else. If our schedules do not permit quality time with our families, then what we are doing is not of God. God will never give us so much to do that we neglect our primary priorities.

God's plan for His children does not include a humdrum, mediocre existence. Life is too precious and too short to be lived that way. The opposite extreme is found in what the world proclaims: Live it up, grab all you can, have a ball—you only go around once!

The Christian's life-style and philosophy bears no resemblance to either of these two extremes. Both modes of living are self-centered; we are God centered.

Knowing our priorities and consciously keeping them in the right order will help our goals fall into place. As a believer in Jesus, we are responsible to God in all things. If we are married, our next priority and responsibility is to our husband or wife. If we have children, their welfare and care will be our third priority. After these three, we have the responsibilities outside our homes and families. These include work, church, other family members, civic interests, and hobbies. It is very easy to slip the number-four priority into the number-one slot and, as a result, be completely out of balance.

Frustration is produced when priorities are out of line. Putting our responsibilities in the proper perspective will make all the difference in the world.

Let's look at some long-range goals (LRG) and some short-range goals (SRG) which may affect our life-styles. Remember: an SRG is application of certain principles and guidelines to our *daily* lives which will bring about the LRG in time.

LRG: To Become Better Organized
SRG: Use a Daily Plan to Schedule Time and Activities

A successful, smooth-running office, business, or home can't be operated in a lackadaisical manner. If certain guidelines are not set down, there will be confusion most of the time. Many people are frustrated because they do not plan.

In discussing how to become better organized, I will use the home as a model. I think most of the difficulty begins and ends here. Regardless of what we do outside our homes, we must first take care of our family's personal needs. This is our primary responsibility.

If you are single and living in an apartment, you have cleaning, laundry, and shopping to do, bills to pay, food to prepare, and so on. The difference between you and the person in the house with five children is that the work load in the house is increased manifold, even though the basic principles are the same.

Make a daily schedule of those things which you need to accomplish that day. I found that making a master schedule for the week helped me begin. We gave the children certain responsibilities, according to their ages and abilities. This is not only a help to Mom and Dad but it is also an important part of their training. This schedule brought out some of our problem areas—areas where we tended to get bogged down—and we worked out solutions for these areas.

When you know basically what has to be done to keep the home neat and clean, and which days are best for particular jobs, you have the first hurdle behind you. A neat house is easier to keep clean. It can only be neat if every person puts away what he has used when he is finished with it. Our homes are a reflection of our personalities and you can tell a lot about a person by going into his home. With a master schedule and a daily routine established, you can move on to the next step.

Business people keep appointment calendars for scheduling their time through the day. These are equally helpful to use at home for scheduling things over and above the daily routine—letters, calls which need to be made, odd jobs, and so on. Keeping a shopping and errand list saves time (and money), too.

Every homemaker and mother has learned to expect the unexpected. Many days just don't turn out the way we had planned. A hundred little things have a way of creeping in to sabotage the best-laid plans. A sense of humor is a must in maintaining a home! All plans need a lot of elasticity.

Housework can be an overwhelming task if you don't know how to stay on top of it. *Hints From Heloise* is a well-known book which gives timesaving hints for running a household.

One time in a seminar, a student confessed that her home was a total wreck. Every room looked like a disaster area. She dramatically pleaded, "What can I do?" All she can do is take one room at a time.

Sift through the junk and throw out everything you haven't used in the last year (excluding true sentimental memorabilia). God is able to clean the closet of your mind, but it is up to you to clean the closets of your home!

Perhaps some of you have the opposite problem. You may be very organized and precise. Life can be difficult for the person who is overly neat and fastidious, because in their eyes everyone else may appear messy and incompetent. This quality may be the reason you are well suited for a job which requires detailed, intricate work, but it is not always easy to live with at home!

We all have our little peculiarities and must learn tolerance in order to live in harmony with ourselves and others. Whether you are too well organized or not organized enough, the key to success lies in your willingness to achieve balance in your life.

LRG: To Know the Joy of a Lifelong Marriage
SRG: Work at Building Your Relationship Every Day

When couples marry, they believe they will have a happy, satisfying, and lasting marriage. The present divorce rate in the United States shows that this is frequently not the case. However, the divorce rate for Christians is estimated at only one in over a thousand marriages.

These are comfortable figures to quote, but from the teaching and counseling I have done, there is more to it than statistics. An intact marriage does not automatically assure happiness. Many couples go through a psychological divorce—existing rather than sharing life together.

A personal relationship with Jesus Christ is the most important element two partners can bring to a marriage. When a man and woman are rightly related to Jesus, they will be rightly related to one another. When God gives us the gift of new life in Christ, we also receive the resources available to love more deeply in our marriages. We may not be able to change the past, but each new day is a new opportunity to love and cherish one another, building the kind of relationship which will last a lifetime.

The shelves of every Christian bookstore are lined with excellent books on marriage. There are books for couples and books written specifically for husbands or wives. It is a rich blessing to have these wonderful books to complement the Bible. I have listed a few in the appendix. If you have a good marriage, read to make it better. If you have problem areas in your marriage, read to learn. When individuals let God's gifts come together in their lives, harmony will develop in their other relationships as well. This is particularly true in marriage.

As persons we are first responsible to God. Our second priority is to the person with whom we have pledged to share our life. Each of these relationships affects the other. If our personal lives are messed up, our marriage will be, too. If our marriage isn't right, we can't be blessed and used of God in other ways.

I believe several basic ideas can be applied to every marriage to bring out the best in one's partner. We already have the most essential element when we have a Christ-controlled life and are spending time daily in prayer and study of the Word. The quality of our lives will be enriched as we evidence the fruit of the Spirit.

Two of the most destructive characteristics to a marriage are selfishness and immaturity. The person who lacks maturity can't see the faults within himself. As conflicts arise, they will not be handled in a mature way. Problems and conflicts do not destroy a marriage, but the way they are handled may prevent them from being resolved. Every problem can be solved if it can be discussed openly and honestly, taking into consideration each person's point of view.

Good communication is the next ingredient. The art of conversation between lovers should be an ever-deepening experience.

What happens to clog the lines of communication after a few years of marriage? In the early years, all we could think about was how wonderful it was to love our beloved, to say and do sweet things as an expression of our love. We overlooked the irritations, tore down the barriers, and shared our feelings from the heart. Has that enemy, selfishness, crept in to block out the joy of giving? Time alone together is the only way to rekindle and restore the intimacy and beauty of love.

The word *love* has taken on many meanings in recent years. Love is for people. We can enjoy, use, and like our possessions, but let's save love for God and people. Love is not a tangible item, but we know of its existence because of its effect. The most beautiful descriptions of love are found in John 3:16 and 1 Corinthians 13:4–7 in the Living Bible.

Many men have been brainwashed by Madison Avenue into thinking that material things are what makes a woman happy. Not so! It's just plain love—kindness, thoughtfulness, understanding, approval, time together. God made us that way. That's the reason He told husbands to love their wives as Christ loves the church.

If your husband lacks these qualities, your life can still begin to blossom as you begin to show this kind of love to him. This is God's kind of love, and He will give it to you as you allow Christ to live and love through you.

LRG: To Have Obedient, Well-Mannered Children
SRG: The Daily Guidance and Training of Your Child

There are so many wonderful books available on discipline, child care, and training that I am not going to attempt to add to what these fine experts have written. All of us need to live in harmonious surroundings, where we know we are loved and accepted for ourselves.

Little people grow up reflecting or reacting to what they see and hear every day. Being a parent is an awesome as well as delightful responsibility. Raising one child or a houseful of children is a joyous, demanding, complex, thrilling, perplexing, funny, expensive, tedious, fascinating, laborious, exhilarating, rich, sacred experience.

Only you can do the best job of raising your child. If you give him life, give him your time and love as well. A nursemaid or child-care center cannot give your child what he needs most—you.

Christians often think they should never have problems with their children. When a Christian has a child with whom he is having difficulty, other Christians are likely to think—and sometimes say, "Well, he must not be doing what he is supposed to do," or "She can tell everyone else what to do, but she can't handle her own family."

False guilt can arise in the parents and they end up having more problems than they started with. In some cases, the parents are at fault and must seek to rectify the error. A Christian counselor's guidance may need to be sought. Please don't allow pride to keep you from admitting that you need help.

But what can we say to the people who make comments about the way we consider our responsibilities? You and your family are the only ones who know the extent of the problems. The casual observer can only judge from what he has seen or heard. If you have a neighbor, friend, or family member who fits into this category, the only thing to do is speak to him in love, assuring him that you are confident his intentions are well meant, but because of his limited view of the situation, he cannot rightly appraise the matter. Let him know you believe it is best for each family, with God's guidance, to work through the events which occur in their lives.

There may be those times, however, when we will need to seek the advice of a Christian friend whose confidence and concern can be relied upon. It can be healthy and helpful to share how God is leading you through a problem. It is often good to receive another person's input. He may have more objectivity toward the situation than you do.

I praise God for the way He has, at particular times, ministered to me through a Christian friend or member of my family. Each individual case must be appraised separately. Caution should be exercised in discussing problems with others. As a general rule, private or intimate details are no one's business but your own.

We want to shield our children from the adversities

and hardships we have faced. We think that somehow they can avoid "growing pains," and can learn at a young age all that it has taken us years of adult life to learn.

Unfortunately, life doesn't work that way. We influence our children in innumerable ways; however, they must learn most of life's lessons on their own.

Two of the most valuable things we can give our children are "roots" and "wings." We try to give them roots—a secure foundation by our love, words, and actions. We trust God to bring them to commitment in Jesus and, when they are on their own, we undergird them daily with our prayers.

Dorothy Law Nolte expresses the needs of children beautifully:

Children Learn What They Live

If a child lives with criticism,
    He learns to condemn.
If a child lives with hostility,
    He learns to fight.
If a child lives with ridicule,
    He learns to be shy.
If a child lives with shame,
    He learns to feel guilty.
If a child lives with tolerance,
    He learns to be patient.
If a child lives with encouragement,
    He learns confidence.
If a child lives with praise,
    He learns to appreciate.
If a child lives with fairness,
    He learns justice.
If a child lives with security,
    He learns to have faith.
If a child lives with approval,
    He learns to like himself.
If a child lives with acceptance and friendship,
    He learns to find love in the world.

To this I can only add:

If a child lives in a Christ-centered home,
  He learns to trust in Jesus early in life.

LRG: To Have Regular, Meaningful Family Devotions
SRG: Set Aside a Few Times Each Week for Informal
Family Worship

If your children are young, it is easy to begin family worship time with Bible stories, songs about Jesus, and simple prayers. As the children get older, it is possible for resistance to set in. Sometimes it takes time to establish personal rapport within a family. Don't become discouraged, and keep your eye on the LRG!

If each person has an opportunity to participate, the devotion time doesn't seem like a sermon. Dad should be the regular leader, but it is wonderful to give each member of the family occasional opportunities to lead a portion of the devotions. Give the children a week's notice to think about and prepare their devotion.

In setting aside a time, take into consideration when each member of the family can be present. For many families, an early breakfast one or two mornings a week is best. Others like to linger around the table after dinner, or sit on the floor in the den or living room. The important thing is to set that time aside and make it a priority.

With young children, you may be able to have family time each night. When children are older and have homework, sports, chores, and added responsibilities, it may only be possible to have one or two times a week together.

Ideally, mealtime is a good time to share the highlights of the day and to relax in fellowship together. For many families, it is the only time they are together all day. I think it is vital to have meals together, even if breakfast has to be very early or dinner a little later than you pre-

fer. If a family cannot find time to eat together, chances
are they have very few other shared interests, either.

LRG: To Serve Christ Through the Work of the Church
SRG: Find an Area of Service

It would be easy to "get involved in church activities."
But that doesn't necessarily denote service. We can conceivably become so busy doing things in our church that
we get out of balance in other areas.

Every church has its backbone of involved members
whose aid can always be counted upon. We need those
saints, but in God's eyes we are all saints; we are all
important to the work of His church. And we all have
areas of service. Some use their skills in finance and
planning; others lend a hand in the kitchen. Some teach
Sunday school, sing in the choir, visit the sick, or help
with charitable causes. Others paint, clip shrubbery, or
maintain a car pool for the elderly. Each of us has a talent
which blends into the entire scope of work and worship
in our church home.

I have a set of cassette tapes called "The Christian
Home" by Dr. Howard Hendricks. He relates an inci-
dent which occurred when he was a young pastor. A lady
in the church enthusiastically assured him that every
time the doors of the church were opened, she and her
family would be there. In his excitement, he shared the
story with his wife, who didn't agree that there was
cause for joy. She told him that if that were true, that
family would have no time to build their personal home
relationships.

Doctor Hendricks cautions us not to expect the church
to do the job which God has given *us* to do. I think that is
wise advice.

LRG: Financial Independence and Security
SRG: Learn to Budget

The parable of the talents is a fine illustration of what God expects of us and how He rewards those who correctly use the gifts He gives us. It is found in Matthew 25:14–30.

A talent is a sum of money, probably worth about a thousand dollars. In this parable, Jesus is teaching that the use we make of the gifts He gives us is vitally important. Each of three slaves was given amounts of money the master felt he could handle. Each was responsible for the proper use of what he was given. The one who was given the least amount did not use what he had been given, but buried it. The other two managed their talents well and were rewarded by being entrusted with more.

God seems to put some leverage on us in the area of finances in order to straighten us out in this and other areas. I have seen many people whose lives were out of balance in several areas and they had continual financial difficulties as well.

God requires balanced priorities. The principle of sowing and reaping (*see* Galatians 6:7)—cause and effect—is always in operation. Wise use of one's income is a sign of inner heart obedience. When money is wasted through frivolous spending, or when other areas of our lives are out of balance, God chastens us in order to turn us again toward responsible, Christian living.

I also know families who carefully use what God has entrusted to them, whose priorities are in order, and whose lives are in balance. They do not have financial difficulties, even when they live on a modest income. It stands to reason that if a person can't handle what he has, God will not give him more.

Financial problems are one of the chief causes of marital conflicts. Many of us are trying to live by the standards of nonbelievers; this doesn't work for the Christian. We often do not let God guide us. We disobey what we know to be truth and try to rationalize our errors. We all possess many things which we do not need. It seems we are trying to satisfy our *greeds* rather than our *needs*.

I do not believe it is a sin to go into debt for a house, an automobile, or a *major* expenditure which is truly needed. Sin comes in the inability to pay the debt. If we live beyond our means or incur debts in bad faith, we are not being good stewards of what God has given us.

We need to learn to budget our income and to live within that budget. I feel the tithe should be the first check written each month. Then we can budget our needs with the remainder.

If you don't know how to correctly manage your finances, I recommend Christian Financial Concepts, Inc., 4730 Darlene Way, Tucker, Georgia 30084. Christian Financial Concepts, Inc. is a nonprofit organization dedicated to sharing God's principles of finance with His people. A list of their materials is available at the above address.

LRG: To Have Good Health and Vitality
SRG: Eat Properly, Get Adequate Rest, and Exercise

If we hope to be physically fit at seventy-five, the time to begin a daily exercise program is now. One of the best all-around exercises is jumping rope! Ten minutes of rope skipping is equivalent to jogging a couple of miles. Walking, biking, jogging, tennis, golf, basic floor exercises, and ballet are all wonderful ways to maintain physical fitness.

A person who is physically active and whose nutritional needs are being met is seldom bored with life. He doesn't want to sit around becoming depressed and lethargic.

If you are not involved in some form of daily exercise, begin with a brisk walk to your doctor's office for a checkup. Ask him for his recommendations on a personal program of physical fitness.

LRG: Personal Growth and Development
SRG: Personal Growth Each Day

As Christians, we want to keep on "growing up in Christ." We want to increase daily our knowledge, wisdom, and understanding of biblical truth.

With that growth comes the desire to continually develop in other areas of our lives. God is interested in the whole person, not just our spiritual development. We will be most effective for Christ when we are well informed on a variety of subjects.

Television is both a marvel and a monster. The world could be evangelized in a matter of weeks through this media. We can watch history in the making and participate in untold numbers of educational pursuits. That's a marvel!

The average American will spend thousands of hours in front of a television set in his lifetime. For the most part, he will watch violence, commercials, and inane trivia. That's a monster! Our brains are like computers; they store all that is seen and heard. It cannot be denied that, in many respects, we are the product of what is programmed into our brains.

If we watched less television, we would read more and have more family conversation and recreation. Personal growth would be stimulated through pursuit of hobbies and creative activities. We will do ourselves and our families a favor if we plan to watch only those programs which will provide some form of enrichment.

We are fortunate today to have a wide variety of opportunities to further our education. The average person does not take full advantage of the public libraries and classes available in most communities. Night classes at local high schools and colleges offer a wide range of subjects at reasonable costs.

Competition is very keen at all levels in the marketplace. Those persons who succeed in their work are those who regularly upgrade their job skills. Seminars seem to be available for every conceivable avenue of learning. With so many advantages available to us, we really have no excuse for not being well versed in the areas where we have an interest.

To summarize, one cannot achieve goals without motivation. What motivates you? What is it within you which causes you to want to move in a new direction? Your motivation will determine your actions.

Every person is born motivated. Through the years, natural motivation is either stifled by circumstances or it is encouraged to develop. When an individual is born again, God gives him His Holy Spirit, who becomes an internal force stimulating his desire to do his best.

Successful businesses, churches, and civic organizations take time to set goals and plan for their needs. Individuals can benefit tremendously from doing the same. Take time to pray and seek God's direction. Use a sheet of paper to brainstorm ideas, goals, and alternatives to see how you can begin to see more positive results in your life.

I would like to encourage married couples to go away together for a weekend alone. Use the time to talk and listen to each other. Share some of your innermost thoughts and feelings about what is important to you. We have to realize that each person has special needs which the other may not possess. Beauty and depth in marriage come when each individual contributes to the union, making their life together better than it could ever be alone.

Anything we learn is good only if we apply it. We can read Scripture and Christian books by the dozen, but if we stifle the working of the Holy Spirit, we will never have the joy of becoming what God created us to be.

Experts in the field of personal development claim

that the average person works only at 50 percent capacity. A job well done gives a person great satisfaction.

If a person's goal is to be self-satisfied, he is chasing after wind. It will never be attained. If his goal is to honor Christ by giving love and happiness to others, he will experience it every day in very real and tangible ways.

12

Using Our Gifts for His Glory

As I was thinking of a title for this final chapter, Mike suggested, "Where Do We Go From Here?" or "Ready—Set—Go!" Suddenly our son, Michael, bounced into the room exclaiming, "I've got it—'Keep on Truckin!'" That sums it up nicely!

My purpose, throughout the book, was to help lay a foundation for you to use to build your life. As God's gifts come together in your life it will truly glorify Him. This is God's purpose for giving us the promises found in Scripture and the power of Jesus to accomplish them. Let's read again 2 Timothy 3:16, 17 in the Amplified Bible:

> Every Scripture *is* God-breathed—given by His inspiration—and profitable for instruction, for reproof *and* conviction of sin, for correction of error *and* discipline in obedience, *and* for training in righteousness [that is, in holy living, in conformity to God's will in thought, purpose and action], so that the man of God may be complete *and* proficient, well-fitted *and* thoroughly equipped for every good work.

Throughout the Bible we are called workers. It is a very high and noble calling to be a worker for the cause of Christ. One may attain fame, wealth, and world renown, but it is of no value compared to knowing Jesus. God redeemed us for a purpose.

> For the grace of God has appeared, bringing salvation to all men, instructing us to deny ungodliness and worldly desires and to live sensibly, righteously and godly in the present age, looking for the blessed

hope and the appearing of the glory of our great God
and Savior, Christ Jesus; who gave Himself for us,
that He might redeem us from every lawless deed
and purify for Himself a people for His own posses-
sion, zealous for good deeds. Titus 2:11–14 (*See also*
James 2:17, 18; 1 Timothy 6:18, 19.)

The work we do and the activities we are involved in
are investments of our lives. How are you investing your
time, talent, and treasure? Do you think God wants to
use you to bring others to Christ?

As Mike turned on the television set the other night to
watch the 10:00 news, the newscaster was reporting a
recent national survey which disclosed that 74 percent of
the people interviewed expressed faith in a Supreme
Being and 24 percent attended church on Sunday. We
both said, "Praise the Lord!" as the following remark
was added: "It seems that a religious revival is beginning to sweep America!"

You and I can play an exciting part in seeing a revival
sweep across our land and around the world. Every
Christian has special talents and abilities to use in sharing the love of Jesus Christ with others. We all have a
ministry and influence in the lives of other people. God
works through His children. He has chosen us and set us
apart as His representatives to an unbelieving world.

I remember many evenings during the mid sixties
through the early seventies, sitting with friends, discussing world and national events and changes which
were being forecast about the direction in which our
nation was headed. We were thankful about some of the
changes so desperately needed and long overdue, such
as discrimination of people because of race, color, or
sex. However, there were other things, such as changing moral values and all the ramifications of the drug
culture, which were frightening and could have terrible
results. In those discussions, I recall saying and hear-

ing, "Well, it will never happen in America!" Somehow those detrimental changes slowly began to come to pass. Then we began to question, "Why don't 'they' do something about it?" But who are "they"—where does one find "them"?

One day a cassette tape came in the mail from Campus Crusade. It was a message recorded by a friend named Howard Ball. On the tape Howard voiced some of these same concerns and proclaimed, "We are 'they'!" Aloud I exclaimed, "Who, me?" How could I be one of them? Surely, 'they' are influential people. They have access to government, corporations, unions, and the mass media. They must be far removed from the life I live. Can Christians who are moral, honest, peace-loving, law-abiding citizens make a difference in the direction our nation is heading?

I began to take inventory by reassessing some values and looking back over the years since I had become a Christian, in order to get a perspective on how God had been leading in my life. Through my childhood and young-adult life, I was pretty shy and reserved. My self-image left much to be desired. Quite frankly, I have often felt just plain insignificant. How could someone such as I make a difference in another person's life or in my country? I thought if I voted in the elections, I had done all I could do. With a list of minus points such as that on my side, where was I headed?

My own life is an example of how God will use a person who is lost, lonely, and defeated, but who has a yearning to know Him and a willingness to learn. Whatever good there is in me is by the gift of God's grace alone.

When I became a Christian, God gave me a hunger to study His Word. After we joined a church, I attended a weekly Bible study and Sunday-school class. Within the first year, I was asked to serve as president of the Sunday-school class and lead the Pioneer Fellowship for

Junior Highs on Sunday evenings. I had never been
president or leader of anything before, but I was thrilled
to be asked and eager to work.

Two years after joining the church, I was asked to substitute for our Sunday-school-class teacher while he was
on vacation. We were surveying the New Testament and
I taught Romans, 1 Corinthians, 2 Corinthians, Galatians,
and Ephesians on five consecutive Sundays. I had never
taught a class of adults before, yet I consented to under-
take the challenge without a moment's hesitation. I did
not look at my own inexperience, but kept my eyes on
Jesus and His enabling power. In fact, it wasn't until
after I had finished teaching the series that I realized I
had never done anything like that before! Soon I taught
the class on a regular basis.

I became active in women's groups and, through the
years, held nearly every position in our church's associa-
tion.

I learned how to share my faith with others and later
an Evangelism Circle was developed. I attended classes
given by Child Evangelism Fellowship and started a
Good News Club in an underprivileged area of the city.

After Mike and I joined the associate staff of Campus
Crusade for Christ in 1972, we were trained by dynamic
Christian pastors and leaders. We learned how to share
our faith with others in informal talks before the public
and began to speak and teach others to do the same. For
two years before moving from Montgomery to Chicago I
taught a Bible study in a nearby Methodist church and
loved sharing how God was working in my life. I saw the
lives of those women begin to blossom. It was one of the
richest experiences of my life.

These things were just the natural outgrowth of love
and gratitude to Jesus. I trusted that the Holy Spirit
would work through me. God uses all things to prepare
us for what lies ahead. As I looked back over the years of
my life with Christ I remembered one day a few months

after I became a Christian. I had knelt in prayer beside our bed and wept with thankfulness for my salvation. I told God I didn't know how He could use someone as ordinary as me, but if He could, I was willing and available. Somehow we get the mistaken notion a person has to be brilliant, outstanding, or important to be used of God, when He only wants faithfulness and availability.

In 1974, I began to teach evangelistic marriage-enrichment seminars. In two and one half years, I taught sixty seminars from coast to coast. There were opportunities to speak in churches, at secular and Christian banquets, and Christian Women's Clubs. I did television, radio, and newspaper interviews.

Since writing my first book, *Totally New*, and this book, I have a heightened desire to work with Christian women, teaching seminars on personal development, marriage, and family living. I know the difference Jesus makes in a life and I want to share it with others.

I am convinced that Christians of all ages are born (again) leaders. You may not think of yourself in that capacity, but you are. As an emissary of Jesus to the world, you are a leader. It doesn't matter if you have a modest income or great wealth, little education or graduate honors. You have a sphere of influence and large numbers of people are affected by your life. God chose to use people, His people, as a means for fulfilling His purposes. This includes you and me—we are "they"! All we have to do is be available to Him.

There is joy, peace, and excitement in serving Christ, but there is also suffering and hardship. I have yet to meet an active Christian who leads an easy life. If we are willing to step out for Christ, we must be willing to bear suffering and endure hardships in His name. I counted the cost and found I would make mistakes, but I couldn't fail, because Jesus promised never to leave me or forsake me.

Beloved, do not be surprised at the fiery ordeal
among you, which comes upon you for your testing,
as though some strange thing were happening to
you; but to the degree that you share the sufferings
of Christ, keep on rejoicing; so that also at the revelation of His glory, you may rejoice with exultation.

1 Peter 4:12, 13

I believe we Christians are destined to live complex
lives. We face alternatives and problems that a non-
Christian doesn't recognize.

A new believer was somewhat perplexed about the
problems in his life since becoming a Christian. He said,
"My life was much easier before I was a Christian. Now I
seem to have problems that were never problems before."

As a non-Christian it didn't bother him to smoke, drink
liquor, speed on the highway, pad his expense account,
or use and hear foul language. But now he is weighing
the whole scope of his life in relation to Christ. The
entire dimension of his life has changed. Instead of looking for temporal results, his life now takes on eternal
importance.

Once his only goal was to be materially successful for
all the worldly reasons. Now he views his position as
significant because God can use his witness for Christ in
the lives of his peers.

Every family, business, and community in America
needs consecrated, godly men and women who will be a
living example of the success and fulfillment found in a
Christ-centered life.

Many of us have practically isolated ourselves from
the world, staying secure and comfortable in our cozy
Christian circles. This last quarter of the twentieth cen-
tury is an exciting time to be alive. Of course, we need to
support one another in prayer and fellowship, but the
time is ripe to become involved in the affairs of our

communities as committed Christians.

Let's check the sphere of influence we have. List all the people with whom you regularly come in contact. Begin with family members, neighbors, close friends, acquaintances, associates at work, and people where you regularly shop. Get a mental picture of these people.

Whether you realize it or not you have an influence on them. It is a staggering thought, isn't it? Do they know you are a Christian? Do you feel free to talk about Jesus with others? Have you ever prayed for God to give you the opportunity to speak about Jesus—how wonderful it is to know you belong to Him and have eternal life? The first time or two, you may just plant a seed of thought in the other person's mind.

In the case of family members, planting seeds may be all you can do. When I was a new believer, I was sure one day I would dramatically lead Mike to Christ. That wasn't in God's plan. My place was to pray for him and let my changed life be an example to him. Those were seeds; others witnessed and showed him the way. Our faithfulness, prayer, and confidence in the work of the Holy Spirit are what is important.

I have heard Christians say they feel their pleasant personality is witness enough, and they would not want to offend someone by telling him about Jesus. That's a cop-out. If our commitment to Christ is genuine and we earnestly want to serve Him, we will be able to say as the Apostle Paul did to the Romans:

> I am under obligation both to Greeks and to barbarians, both to the wise and to the foolish. Thus, for my part, I am eager to preach the gospel to you also who are in Rome. For I am not ashamed of the gospel, for it is the power of God for salvation to every one who believes, to the Jew first and also to the Greek.
>
> Romans 1:14–16

Hearts are prepared and waiting to hear (*see* John 4:35).

After sharing my faith with someone, I am amazed at how often they say, "Thank you. You will never know how I have been searching and hoping someone would tell me about Jesus." I have even had people say they had prayed God would send someone to tell them how they could know Jesus.

The first year I taught marriage seminars, over one thousand women indicated they had prayed to invite Christ into their lives. Most of those women did not attend a church or own a Bible, yet God had prepared their hearts. With tears in their eyes, they would hug me, saying, "Thank you." It is wonderful to have the confidence that the Holy Spirit indwells those who are saved, and that the results of their lives are in His hands (*see* 1 Thessalonians 5:23, 24).

I haven't seen the lovely lady who took me to her Sunday-school class since we bought her house and she moved from the city. But I have thanked God for her a thousand times. Perhaps you, too, will share your faith with a stranger and never see him again. But I guarantee he will never forget you! Sure, God could have used any number of ways to introduce me to Jesus, but He chose one of His children—and she was willing.

Last summer when Mike's parents were visiting, his mother and I went to our local Christian Women's Club luncheon. We found a table and introduced ourselves to the other ladies already seated. One young woman smiled and said, "Yes, I know who you are. Last year my friend dragged me to a luncheon, and you were the speaker. I accepted Jesus that day. My life has been so wonderful this year; I'm just glad to see you again and say thanks." So, you see, you never know!

Occasionally there are days when I am very tired and begin to wonder if the results are really worth all the effort. At these times a call or letter will come from a woman who has received Christ. She will share how her life has changed and marriage improved. God will use her to minister to me and my joy will again be full. I know that this is God's work for me.

Many of you will share your faith in the quiet living room of a friend or neighbor. Hopefully, you will be able to help guide and disciple them. It is so beautiful to explore God's Word with a new sister or brother in Christ.

As you list the people within your sphere of influence, begin to pray for them. Remember this passage from Romans 10:14, 15 in the Living Bible:

But how shall they ask him to save them unless they believe in him? And how can they believe in him if they have never heard about him? And how can they hear about him unless someone tells them? And how will anyone go and tell them unless someone sends him? That is what the Scriptures are talking about when they say, "How beautiful are the feet of those who preach the Gospel of peace with God and bring glad tidings of good things." In other words, how welcome are those who come preaching God's Good News!

To know Jesus Christ is life's greatest experience. Don't keep it a secret. Go—tell others, so they, too, may receive our Savior and experience the joy of living in harmony with their Creator.

If Christians are going to have an impact for Jesus on this generation, the quality of our lives must reflect the attributes of our Savior. We must have love and unity within the Body of Christ, and exhibit genuine care and concern for one another.

Remember the inscription on the plaque which hangs on our kitchen wall?

WHAT YOU ARE IS GOD'S GIFT TO YOU . . .
WHAT YOU MAKE OF YOURSELF IS
YOUR GIFT TO GOD

Our gift to God comes through the way we respond to and utilize the gifts He has given us. If we do not allow the Holy Spirit full access to every area of our lives, we cannot experience the power available to us as Christians.

I believe you have a creative potential far above your dreams or expectations. I pray you will strive toward it, work for it, and experience in life all that God created for you. Concentrate on your future. Begin to look at all the positive aspects of your life in Christ. Keep your heart and mind open and be willing to learn how to let God's gifts come together in your life.

May the Lord bless and protect you; may the Lord's face radiate with joy because of you; may he be gracious to you, show you his favor, and give you his peace.

Numbers 6:24–26 LB

Appendix A
Scripture References
on Attributes and Attitudes

Charity; 1 Tim. 1:5; Rom. 15:1

Chastity; 1 Thess. 4:3; Deut. 5:18

Cheerfulness; Prov. 17:22, 15:13

Comfort; 2 Cor. 1:3, 4; Prov. 29:17

Contentment; Prov. 15:16; Phil. 4:11

Courage; Ps. 118:6; Deut. 31:6

Courtesy; Col. 4:6; 1 Pet. 3:8

Discernment; 1 Cor. 2:14; Heb. 5:14

Encouragement; 1 Thess. 5:11; Heb. 3:13

Earnestness; Deut. 6:5; Ps. 119:2

Expressions of good; Ps. 100:2, 147:1

Faith; Heb. 11:1; 1 John 5:4

Friendship; Prov. 17:17; Phil. 1:3

Frugality; John 6:12; Prov. 21:20

Fruitfulness; Phil. 1:11; Col. 1:10

Gentleness; James 3:17; 2 Tim. 2:24

Gratitude; Heb. 13:15; 1 Pet. 2:9

Hope; 1 John 3:3; 1 Pet. 1:3

Humility; Isa. 57:15; John 4:10

Innocence; 1 Tim. 1:5; Rev. 14:5

Uncharitableness; 1 Tim. 6:4; Isa. 29:20

Impurity; Rom. 1:24; 1 Cor. 6:18

Despondency; Prov. 17:22, 15:13

Misery; Ps. 107:17; Rom. 2:9

Discontent; Prov. 19:3; Phil. 2:14

Fear; Isa. 66:4, 33:14

Discourtesy; Prov. 18:23; 1 Kings 12:13

Dullness; Luke 12:56; Ps. 92:6

Discouragement; Ps. 73:2, 3; Prov. 13:12

Indifference; Isa. 47:8; Heb. 2:3

Repressions of evil; Ps. 39:1; Col. 3:5

Unbelief; John 12:37; Heb. 3:12

Unfriendliness; Ps. 142:4; Luke 15:16

Waste; Prov. 12:27, 18:9

Unfruitfulness; Matt. 3:10, 13:22

Vindictiveness; Acts 23:12; Ps. 27:12

Ingratitude; Rom. 1:21; John 10:32

Despair; Eph. 2:12; Eccles. 2:17

Pride; Prov. 29:23, 16:18

Guilt; Ps. 38:4, 51:3

157

Appendix B
Suggested Reading List

Can Your Child Read? Is He Hyperactive?, William G. Crook, M.D.;
    Pedicenter Press, P.O. Box 3116, Jackson, Tenn. 38301
Let's Eat Right and Keep Fit, Adelle Davis; Signet Books
Let's Have Healthy Children, Adelle Davis; Signet Books
Dare to Discipline, James Dobson; Tyndale House
Hide or Seek, James Dobson; Revell
What Wives Wish Their Husbands Knew About Women, James Dob-
    son; Tyndale House
Why Your Child Is Hyperactive, Ben F. Feingold, M.D.; Random
    House
Forever My Love, Margaret Hardisty; Harvest House
Heaven Help the Home, Howard Hendricks; Victor Books
God's Key to Health and Happiness, Elmer A. Josephson; Revell
The Act of Marriage, Beverly and Tim LaHaye; Zondervan
How to Be Happy Though Married, Tim LaHaye; Tyndale House
The Total Woman, Marabel Morgan; Revell
Let's Try Real Food, Ethel H. Renwick; Zondervan
Improving Your Child's Behavior Chemistry, Lendon Smith, M.D.;
    Prentice-Hall
How to Feed Your Hyperactive Child, George E. Stoner and Laura
    J. Stevens; Doubleday
The Holy Spirit: Who He Is and What He Does, R. A. Torrey; Revell
The Power of Prayer, R. A. Torrey; Zondervan
Emotional Health and Nutrition, Carlson Wade; Award Books
Intended for Pleasure, Ed Wheat, M.D., and Gaye Wheat; Revell
Do Yourself a Favor: Love Your Wife, H. Page Williams; Logos
Communication—Key to Your Marriage, H. Norman Wright; Regal
    Books

159